UNLEASHED

STORIES FROM ALL SAINTS' BOOVAL

Compiled by
JOHN ARNOLD AND HEATHER WOOD

Copyright © 2021

JF Arnold Publications

ISBN

Paperback: 978-0-6451473-0-8

ePub: 978-0-6451473-1-5

All rights reserved.

No part of this book may be reproduced in any form or by any electronic or mechanical means, including information storage and retrieval systems, without written permission from the author, except for the use of brief quotations in a book review.

We pay our respect to Aboriginal Elders past, present and future and extend that respect to other First Nations people. Aboriginal and Torres Strait Islander readers are advised that this book may contain images of people who have died.

 A catalogue record for this book is available from the National Library of Australia

Scriptures marked NIV taken from the Holy Bible, New International Version®, NIV®. Copyright © 1973, 1978, 1984, 2011 by Biblica, Inc.™ Used by permission of Zondervan. All rights reserved worldwide. www.zondervan.com The "NIV" and "New International Version" are trademarks registered in the United States Patent and Trademark Office by Biblica, Inc.™

Scriptures and additional materials marked TEV are from the Good News Bible © 1994 published by the Bible Societies/HarperCollins Publishers Ltd UK, Good News Bible© American Bible Society 1966, 1971, 1976, 1992. Used with permission.

Scripture marked NKJV taken from the New King James Version®. Copyright © 1982 by Thomas Nelson. Used by permission. All rights reserved.

Scripture marked RSV is from the Revised Standard Version of the Bible, copyright 1952 [2nd edition, 1971] by the Division of Christian Education of the National Council of the Churches of Christ in the United States of America. Used by permission. All rights reserved.

CONTENTS

Foreword   vii
Archbishop of Brisbane

Preface   ix
Photographs   xiii

1. The Rev Colin and Mrs Judith Ware   1
2. Mrs Judith Ware   4
3. The Rev Don and Mrs Margaret Douglass   10
4. Mrs Margaret Douglass   13
5. The Rev Jim Stonier, Curate 1963-1966   22
    Photographs   31
6. Les and Elaine Vincent, Bob and Olive Robertson, and Brian and Miriam Chantrill   34
7. Jim Holbeck   39
8. Ivory (Shield) Shields   47
9. Greg and Del (Holbeck) Ezzy   58
10. Kathy (Mitchell) Robinson   65
11. Grahame and Sally (Saunders) Stephens   70
12. Lesley (McGrath) Woodley   73
13. Tom and Heather (Rasmussen) Wood   79
14. John McNamee   95
15. June Singleton   101
16. Bill and Hilary Saunders   107
17. Patricia Frith   110
18. Doug Wiskar   112
19. Alan and Beth Woolard   114
20. Ian McGrath   120
21. Frank and Merle Savage   127

*This book is dedicated to
Judith Ware and Margaret Douglass
through whom the grace of God worked
to enable, support and augment
the faithful ministry of their husbands
the Rev Colin Ware and the Rev Don Douglass.*

FOREWORD

ARCHBISHOP OF BRISBANE

I welcome this volume compiled by John Arnold and Heather Wood, which gathers together the faith journeys of its various contributors, which had their beginning in All Saints' Booval in the late 1950s and early 1960s.

Under the inspired leadership of the Reverend Colin Ware (1955-1960) and the Reverend Don Douglass (1961-1965), those days are recalled with great fondness in this volume.

Colin Ware and Don Douglass's ministries set the course for many people in dedicating their lives to Christ and serving Christ's mission.

The seeds of faith were sown on fertile ground and a rich harvest of willing workers in Christ's name was the result.

We can look back at this time in our history as a time of great spiritual awakening for many people.

They heard the call to dedicate their lives to Christ and have continued to do so over the decades since.

I pray that our churches today may bear similar fruit, that God will continue to raise up willing workers for the spread of the gospel and that the harvest will be as plentiful as in days gone by.

May God continue to bless us in the ministries to which we have been called.

 'To God be the glory, great things he has done.'

Yours in Christ,
+ Phillip Brisbane
The Most Reverend Dr Phillip Aspinall
Archbishop of Brisbane

PREFACE

The decade 1955 to 1965 was one of extraordinary spiritual growth and blessing at All Saints' Booval. Many people experienced new life in Christ and the renewing power of the Holy Spirit and were unleashed to serve God both in the local community and in the wider world. That is why this collection of their stories recalling that era and the ripples that have radiated out from All Saints' over the past sixty years, is called *Unleashed – Stories from All Saints' Booval*. This publication coincides with the 125th anniversary of All Saints' Church in 2021.

We wish to thank all who have assisted in bringing this book to birth - especially those who have contributed their stories and photos, the Archives of the Diocese of Southern Queensland and of the Church Missionary Society for historical information and Belinda Pollard for assistance with publishing. Unfortunately many of the old photos are blurry or scratched, but we hope they are clear enough to recapture the past.

We apologise to any whom we were unable to contact for their story. Of course, God's blessing has always been on the Parish and many more stories could be told by people unleashed for God's mission during its many eras.

Unleashed – Stories from All Saints' Booval opens with recollections from the widows of the first two Rectors after the Parish attained independent status in August 1959. Mrs Judith Ware and Mrs Margaret Douglass are now in their nineties and the book is dedicated to them.

Their husbands, the Rev Colin Ware (Vicar and then Rector 1955 - 1960) and the Rev Don Douglass (Rector 1961 - 1965), were both ex-servicemen, Colin having been wounded in Egypt and Don having been a POW in Germany. They came to Booval with a deep love for Christ and for people and a desire to see men and women, boys and girls converted, discipled and unleashed for God's mission in the world.

The Rev Don Douglass expressed the Parish Vision in his 1963 Annual Report to the Parish:

> Mission is the purpose of the Church's existence. Each organization and all we do must be geared to this end…. Our Lord calls us to himself, then sends us out. His commission to the church is quite clear and the promise of His power, His presence and the Holy Spirit is given that we might witness to His death and resurrection and power to save.

The report went on to stress the importance of equipping the congregation to be a team committed to Jesus, each other and the world around them:

> Not the clergy alone, but the clergy and the people are the 'laos' – "the people of God". Our prior need is not finance or buildings but men and women who know Christ and are out to serve Him. There are unlimited jobs to be done, people waiting to be reached. We need Christian leaders, dedicated and committed, ready to be trained to reach and teach others.

Highlights during the decade included three week-long evangelistic Parish missions with evening meetings for youth and adults and afternoon meetings for children. The first mission was led by Captain Roy Buckingham of the Church Army in November 1957, the second by the Rev Jim Payne, Rector of St Stephen's Coorparoo in November 1961 and the third by Bishop Clive Kerle, Bishop of Armidale, in April 1964. Another highlight was the establishment of Griffith House in Ipswich, a half-way house for people transitioning into society from Wacol Mental Hospital. It was officially opened early in 1965. Yet another highlight was the number of League of Youth camps at which young people made life-changing faith commitments to Christ. Pastoral visiting, promoting daily Bible reading in the home, intercessory prayer, cross-cultural mission and nurturing children through CEBS, GFS, and RE programs in the schools were Parish priorities.

Before long families were responding to God's call to serve in Aboriginal communities in North Australia and others began courses to prepare for the ordained ministry and missionary service. Most continued within the Anglican Church but some moved out into other denominations. *Unleashed – Stories from All Saints' Booval* reveals the diverse pathways that they took, some in medicine and nursing, some in pastoral ministry, some in education, others in community development and management, but all for the advance of God's kingdom. The stories also convey the personal cost of following Christ, a reminder that when Jesus called on his disciples to take up their cross and follow Him, He really meant it. There have been setbacks and suffering along the way, but their testimony is that their struggles and "hanging in for the long haul" have all been worth it for the glory of Christ.

A common theme in the stories is the writers' indebtedness and gratitude to All Saints' Booval for the faith foundations laid for a life unleashed for God's service. Here they learned that God loved them, that Christ died for them and that the Holy Spirit indwelt and empowered them. They discovered their identity through belonging to Christ and His Church and that "God's service is perfect freedom".

It is the prayer of the compilers and contributors that all who read *Unleashed – Stories from All Saints' Booval* will praise God for all that He has done and rejoice that Jesus is the same yesterday, today and forever.

John Arnold and Heather Wood
Co-Editors

All Saints' Anglican Church Booval early 1960s

All Saints' Booval Youth Camp early 1960s. (1) Margaret Douglass with Helen; (2) Heather Rasmussen; (3) Ivory Shield; (4) Ken Rose; (5) Kathy Mitchell; (6) Judith Douglass; (7) Grahame Stephens; (8) Greg Ezzy; (9) Ian Douglass; (10) Jim Holbeck.

1

THE REV COLIN AND MRS JUDITH WARE

THEIR LIFE JOURNEYS IN BRIEF

Rev Colin and Mrs Judith Ware

COLIN LESLIE GEORGE WARE WAS BORN ON 2 DECEMBER 1917 and grew up in the Brisbane suburb of Kelvin Grove. His family were typical of many Australians at that time, battling with poverty. Times were tough when Colin left school in 1930 in the midst of the Depression. However, Colin was blessed with good mathematical skills and was fortunate to find employment in Carrick's furniture factory near the Grey St Bridge. He came from a nominal Church of England family and was not used to attending church. A work mate at the factory shared his Christian faith with Colin during a lunch break and Colin was converted to faith in Christ. He said it was like coming out of darkness into the light. Colin entered St Francis' College at the beginning of WWII to train for the Anglican priesthood but abandoned the course to enlist in the AIF. His regiment sailed to the Middle East on *The Queen Mary*. Initially he was in the medical corps to alleviate the fears of his parents regarding his safety. However, this relatively safe position did not sit well with Colin while men were being killed or coming back from the front badly wounded. So he transferred to the front line as a stretcher-bearer. After being at El-Alamein just a few months, Colin was severely injured in both feet and had to be repatriated. After a long period of convalescence, Colin completed his theological studies and was ordained in Melbourne. For ten years he served in Anglican brotherhoods, first in the slums of Footscray, Melbourne 1946-1947, then as a Mission Chaplain in Brisbane assisting Canon WPB Miles 1947-1950. Canon Miles was a legendary figure noted for his frugal lifestyle and commitment to mission. Colin then served as Rector of Mossman in North Queensland 1950-1955 where he oversaw the completion of the beautiful Byzantine stone St David's Church in 1952.

Judith Patricia Mearns was born in Roma Queensland in 1928 and grew up in Annerley, Brisbane where she attended St Philip's Anglican Church Thompson Estate. She was educated at Junction Park State School Annerley and St Aiden's School Corinda. After training as a Nursing Sister at Saint Martin's Hospital Brisbane, she worked in the Kilcoy Hospital and then Mossman District Hospital.

Colin and Judith Ware met in Mossman and were married at All Saints' Booval on 2 January 1956 soon after Colin had been instituted as Vicar there. Colin and Judith served together at Booval (Brisbane)1955-1960, Newtown (Sydney) 1961-1965, Chaplain Gladesville Psychiatric Hospital (Sydney) 1965-1970, Villawood (Sydney) 1970-1973, Wilcannia (NSW with BCA) 1973-1974, Pine Rivers-Petrie (Brisbane) 1974-1978, Norman Park (Brisbane)1981-1990. Colin and Judith lived in retirement at Nambour where Colin died on 6 July 1997. Judith Ware remained at Nambour until 2015 and now lives at Rothwell Queensland.

Colin and Judith Ware had five children - William, Elspeth, Kingsley, Hillary and Timothy.

2

MRS JUDITH WARE

RECOLLECTIONS OF COLIN'S AND HER MINISTRY AT ALL SAINTS' BOOVAL
1955-1960

| Mrs Judith Ware 2020

(With assistance from her son, Kingsley Ware)

DURING THE EARLY YEARS OF THE SECOND WORLD WAR, Colin Ware felt keenly that he should play his part with Australian young men fighting overseas. He could have stayed home from the war since he was studying theology at the time, but he refused to take that option. On one occasion, while pastoral visiting, he came to a home where the mother had just received news of her soldier son's death overseas. Watching her grief and feeling the reality of her son's sacrifice had a deep impact on Colin's thinking. He renounced his right to stay home and enlisted.

He never felt that he could bear arms but neither did he want a safe position. So he took on the dangerous role of a stretch bearer on the front line. It wasn't long before he was severely injured in the battle of El-Alamein in Egypt in October 1942 and he was repatriated home with wounds in both feet. It was some time after the war had ended in 1945 that Colin was released from military hospital and able to walk again but needing surgical boots for the rest of his life.

He always thanked God for the gift of being able to walk again. His constant desire was to visit in the parish on foot – when he could have taken the car. Dressed in the black shirt and crosses of an Anglican priest, he saw significant value in the visual presence of a minister in the everyday world. This opened the way to talk with people about matters of faith that in turn strengthened his ministry. Converted in his mid-teens, faith in Jesus had transformed his life and Colin wanted others to know the Truth. Because he had been to the Second World War and had been on the front line as a stretcher bearer, many people respected him for this.

Colin had grown up during the Great Depression in a family that at times went without sufficient food, heating or general stability. This gave him an understanding of how to live frugally and enabled him to identify with people in his parish who were battlers. This also meant he was careful with church funds. Although he received his full stipend during the Booval days, this was not a deciding factor in whether or not he would accept a parish appointment. In later years he worked in several places where he had to rely on his military pension to survive.

Colin and I were engaged not long before Colin accepted the call to Booval in late 1955. We were married on January 2, 1956 and so I joined Colin in parish life. Colin was the third incumbent since Booval had been separated from Ipswich parish in 1951.

Colin was passionate about his faith and about visiting. Colin visited every house in the Parish. He would door-knock a whole street at a time, visiting every house. His goal was to bring people to faith in the Lord. To assist folk in their spiritual journey, he would invite them to church. In those days there was usually someone at home during the day and most were willing at least to open the door. People were generally respectful if not interested. However, a number of people responded to this contact and started coming to church.

One family's story remains clear to this day - the family of Olive and Bob Robertson. Olive had had some form of Christian upbringing but Bob had had none. After a visit by Colin, Bob responded to his down-to-earth, real, ordinary personality. The Robertsons started coming to church and soon became staunch parishioners. In time they went to the mission field (CMS) in the Northern Territory where they started to raise their family. In due course they returned to Booval and continued at All Saints'. Later they moved to Sydney but always retained their faith.

There were a number of smaller active Anglican Centres in the parish with regular services at Bundamba, Dinmore, Redbank and Goodna. They didn't all have a weekly service but Colin visited them at least fortnightly or monthly. Colin took multiple services every Sunday – three or four depending on the Sunday of the month.

Colin had Sunday Schools at each Centre, staffed by faithful parishioners, and these proved to be very popular. Sunday School was not likely to be used for 'baby-sitting' since most children had to get themselves to the church by walking. Sometimes the parents came with their children. Colin saw Sunday School as an integral part of the faith development of the parish and it was often run at a different time to the church service.

After a few years in the Parish, the Sunday School children were growing into young adults and many became fully fledged church members. There was a thriving Youth Group in the parish led by parishioners. This really helped young people grow in their faith and so they weren't lost, but rather transitioned from Sunday School to church. There was also a youth group in the Brisbane Anglican Diocese, drawing young people together from many different parishes. This was the League of Youth affiliated with the

Church Missionary Society. It was evangelical in focus and some men from this group later became ordained ministers.

The Billy Graham Crusade was held in Brisbane in 1959. Colin had great respect for this ministry but it is hard to remember how much impact it had in the parish.

Colin taught Religious Education in the schools on a weekly basis. He taught in all the State Schools within the Parish boundaries, both primary and high school. Through this he had an immediate and positive contact with the children. Colin had a likeable personality and children responded to him. He wasn't highbrow (as many adults in positions of authority were in those days) and children could talk with him. They in turn spoke with their parents about 'Vicar Ware'. Whenever a child responded to his teaching, Colin would contact the parents. Often the parents had already come to know Colin through his house-to-house ministry and some would come to church. Of course, some only stayed a few weeks but others made a connection and so continued on their faith journey.

Colin also regularly ministered to the inmates of the then Goodna Mental Hospital. In those days many people spent their entire lives within the confines of the hospital and in many ways were cut off from society. Colin was deeply concerned about their plight and sought to give them all the spiritual assistance that he could.

| Rev Colin Ware 1960s

The original All Saints' Church had a large vacant block of land behind it. Since the Sunday School was now so large, a second hall was needed to cater for the younger grades and this was constructed behind the existing hall. Behind this, a second building was constructed - a rectory to house the minister's family. Colin was keen for this to happen so that the church no longer had to pay rent for the rectory and so that the minister could now live on the church grounds. All these buildings were paid for before Colin and I left the parish. The rectory that they built was typical of the houses in the area, neither extravagant nor skimpy. This building program occurred in the middle years of our time at Booval.

Colin always kept the church grounds tidy. He wanted the house of the Lord to look neat and attractive. He enjoyed the physical labour involved and saw this as a release from the pressures of parish ministry. His willingness to be involved in the physical work of a church increased his contact and rapport with the parishioners. Colin did not cling to position or privilege but embraced the mundane responsibilities of his role. One Christmas holiday season the church interior was painted by a group of volunteers and then the exterior was painted by professionals.

While Colin was fully focussed on the parish, I was busy at home with our two young children. Towards the end of our time at Booval, when the children were a little older, I was able to teach a senior Sunday School class which I enjoyed.

Colin was sincere, approachable and passionate. People came to respect him, enjoy his company and respond to his teaching. He had his own private devotions in the church daily usually saying Morning and Evening Prayer.

In his ministry, Colin always sought to honour the Lord but especially at festival times like Easter, Christmas, and Mother's Day. He scorned the commercialisation of these seasons and taught with passion their true and underlying meaning. He was evangelistic in his presentation of the Christian faith. The church was not to be a comfortable club.

Colin preached with feeling, vigour, passion and sincerity. The Gospel was alive. Jesus was real. Faith was something strong and tough to hold onto. In his sermons he sought to give people a phrase or an idea or a text to hold on to, to take out into the week.

He often illustrated his sermons with stories usually from his own life experience. To Colin there was nothing dry about Christianity.

After five years of ministry, Colin was exhausted. He had given it his all and felt, by his own persuasion, that he had nothing left to give. This was very typical of Colin. He went into a new parish with great energy and passion, gave it his all and then moved on.

Colin's farewell sermon, preached at All Saints' in October 1960, was inspired by 2 Corinthians 3:18 (RSV):

> "And we all, with unveiled face, beholding the glory of the Lord, are being changed into his likeness from one degree of glory to another; for this comes from the Lord who is the Spirit."

3

THE REV DON AND MRS MARGARET DOUGLASS

THEIR LIFE JOURNEYS IN BRIEF

| Rev Don and Mrs Margaret Douglass early 1960s

DONALD MARSH DOUGLASS WAS BORN IN SYDNEY ON 7 MAY 1919 and his family lived in Beecroft. In 1924 they moved to London where Don's father managed the London branch of the Queensland Insurance Company. They lived in Sutton, Surrey and

Don was educated at Homefield Preparatory School and, for his final school years, at Epsom College. He visited Australia with his mother in 1928. In his teen years he joined the Crusaders, a Christian youth group, where he came to a personal faith in Christ. He left school at 17 and worked for several years for the New Zealand Insurance Company.

World War II was declared in August 1939 and the following January Don was called up and joined the Fifth Battalion of the Wiltshire Regiment. His brother Peter, a pilot in the RAF, died of wounds after being shot down over Belgium in May 1940. In 1942 Don volunteered to join the 2nd Airborne Division, was commissioned as a Second Lieutenant and was proud of the wings and red beret he wore as a member of the Parachute Regiment. After serving in North Africa and Italy, he was relocated back to England. In September 1944, Lieutenant Don Douglass parachuted into Holland as part of a ploy to secure the Arnhem Bridge over the Nederrijn River for advancing British troops. The troops were delayed and after four days of bitter fighting Don was captured by the German Army and transferred to the Olaf 79 POW Officers' Camp near Brunswick (Braunschweig) in Germany. Here he remained until he was liberated by the American GIs on 12 April 1945. He was discharged from the British Army in September 1946 after nearly seven years in uniform.

The Douglass family returned to Australia and settled in Mosman NSW. Don entered Medical School at the University of Sydney in 1947 but abandoned the course after four years. He then heard God's call to the ordained ministry and after studying theology for two years at Moore College, was ordained deacon in February 1954 and priest in December the same year.

Margaret Ida Prescott was born on 25 May 1928 in Mill Hill, London. The family sailed to Australia, arriving in Sydney in January 1932. The family lived in suburbs on the North Shore, settling in Cremorne. Margaret was educated at the Christian Science "Hillcrest" School at Wollstonecraft from 1933 to 1937, Mosman Primary School (1938-1939), Neutral Bay Intermediate High School (1940-1942), SCEGGS Darlinghurst (1943-1945) and Sydney University Arts Faculty (1946-1948). Margaret came to a personal faith in Christ at an ISCF Camp at Mt Victoria in January 1942 and grew in her faith through belonging to St Augustine's Neutral Bay, Crusaders and the Sydney University Evangelical Union.

Margaret taught English and Mathematics at SCEGGS Moss Vale 1949, Abbotsleigh, Wahroonga 1950-1951 and St Catherine's, Waverley 1952-1953. Later she resumed teaching at Queenwood, Mosman 1971-1973 and became the founding Principal of St Luke's Secondary School Dee Why from 1974 to 1987. The family home was in Chatswood during these years.

Don Douglass and Margaret Prescott were married on 4 January 1950. Margaret later wrote, "I should have known when I married a man who had volunteered to jump out of aeroplanes, that life was not going to be quite straight-forward." (*We're Here Now...* p 203). They served together in ministry in three Australian dioceses. Don was Curate in Charge of Asquith/Berowra (Sydney) 1954-1956, Rector of Port Hedland (NW Australia) 1956-1961, Booval (Brisbane) 1961-1965, Cremorne /Neutral Bay (Sydney) 1965-1970 and Chaplain at Macquarie (Psychiatric) Hospital, North Ryde (Sydney) 1970-1984. Their retirement home was in Leura in the Blue Mountains.

Don and Margaret had four children - Ian, Judith, Helen and Michael. The Reverend Donald Douglass died on 10 June 2003 at the age of 84. Mrs Margaret Douglass lives in Castle Hill NSW.

4

MRS MARGARET DOUGLASS

REFLECTIONS ON DON'S AND HER MINISTRY AT ALL SAINTS' BOOVAL
1961-1965

ADAPTED FROM MARGARET AND DON DOUGLASS AUTOBIOGRAPHY *WE'RE HERE NOW, SO MAKE THE BEST OF IT,* (SYDNEY: CENTRE FOR THE STUDY OF AUSTRALIAN CHRISTIANITY, 1998) CHAPTER 21

| Rev Don and Mrs Margaret Douglass 1992

DON AND I LOOKED BACK ON OUR YEARS AT BOOVAL AS perhaps the happiest and the most personally rewarding of all our years of Christian ministry. We both grew in our love and understanding of God in a special way through the people and the situations in which we found ourselves. We felt it was a little like being back in the time of 'The Acts'. In spite of our lack of abilities, people were being converted almost every week. The Church was growing and there was a wonderful family 'belongingness' among us. The Church family shared both the serious and the fun sides of life.

Don accepted and respected the people as they were and they accepted his clear gospel message. We saw many come to Jesus for the first time and many grow in their knowledge and love of Him. The parish work increased greatly as people responded to the message of God's love in Jesus and, for the first time, a number of daytime Bible studies were started in homes. God had prepared the parish for our coming through the faithfulness of the Rev Colin Ware who had been the Rector before Don. He had discovered afresh the wonder of the Scriptures and heard for the first time of the Scripture Union. He spent the last months of his time at Booval visiting the homes and asking people to join Scripture Union and read the Bible daily. Jeff Roper, the Queensland CMS General Secretary, with his wife Ursula, had been the means of introducing a number of the Booval youth to Jesus. It was because these young people's lives had so reflected their new personal faith that the parish nominators asked Jeff to recommend a name for the new Rector.

As the work grew the Parish Council decided a Curate was needed. A house was built in the grounds next to the Rectory and we were delighted when Jim Stonier joined us. Jim was single and so spent a lot of time with us at the Rectory. He was a real blessing in the parish particularly among the youth. When he knew us well enough, he told us that on the day of his interview for the job, our two boys had been flicking gravel from the drive through the window onto his back. Don was blissfully unaware as Jim tried to sit sedately and answer enthusiastically while, at the same time, ignoring what was happening to his back. With Jim or someone else constantly at the Rectory and Don and I each busy with our commitments, we had very little time together. I resented this and one day rang Don from a public phone asking for an appointment to see him to discuss Mothers' Union! I hoped he would get the message. He made an appointment for Friday at 11 am after I taught Bremer High Scripture. We (Jim, Don and I) were just finishing morning tea and I got up to go to the study for my appointment, when the doorbell rang and one of the parishioners was there to see Don. He ushered her into the study and I was left fuming. I don't think we ever did have that appointment. He did, though, arrange for Jim to look after the children so he could take me out to dinner in Brisbane and to the ballet for my thirty-fifth birthday. That night out was a wonderful but very rare treat. We did not talk about Mothers' Union.

The parish had six centres – Booval, Bundamba, Dinmore, Riverview, Redbank and Goodna. All Saints' Booval had three services each Sunday – 6.20 am, 7.15 am (both Holy Communion) and 7 pm Evening Prayer. I still can hardly believe that I managed to get to that 6.20 am service. The other centres all had two services a month and an old parish paper I found listed 25 meetings each month at which either Don or I were meant to be present. We had only been in the parish for four weeks and already Don had me teaching Scripture at Bremer High while he himself taught at five primary schools. We were immediately back to the frantically busy parish life we had experienced in our first parish but this time there was a big and very supportive congregation with which to work.

Remembering the success of the Young Wives group in that parish and realising the very large number of young families in the area, I invited Professor Rendle-Short, the Professor of Child Care at Queensland University, to be the first speaker at a new Booval Young Wives group. The enthusiasm of the young wives was great and the meetings were to become, for many of us, the high times of our month. We managed to get outstanding speakers and, at the same time, to have lots of fun. We formed a tennis club and our children played together, so that increasingly much of our family lives were centred around the Church. I was really very, very, happy. I had made so many lovely friends.

...We received many encouraging letters and kept in touch with a number of dear friends from Booval. Ida, one of the 'Young Wives', (who died at the age of 63 in 1994 as a shining Christian) wrote on 16 March, 1965 –

Dear Margaret,

...I know that it has been through your wonderful Christian fellowship and through your guidance and your prayers that I have come to know the Lord Jesus as my personal Saviour and Lord. I must confess before knowing you, it had never ever entered my head or my heart that I actually had to ask the Lord Jesus into my heart and ask Him to stay there so I could do His will. This has been and still is, the greatest event of my life, Margaret, and I am sure you will agree with me it is impossible to sum this up in two words, 'Thank you'.

Sincerely yours
Ida

Rev Don and Mrs Margaret Douglass with Helen (top R), Front L to R Ian and Judith Douglass and Bruce Tennant early 1960s

I have always felt in a parish that the organisations should be run by the people rather than the minister or his wife, and so, although I was very busy attending all the meetings in the parish at this time, I was no longer leading them. A number of the Young Wives, fearfully and reluctantly at first, and then with confidence and real God-given ability, had taken on leadership in a number of the organisations.

The young people's work was particularly encouraging. I remember one house-party at Mt Tamborine when Vic Smith was the speaker. We had been on a long hike – it was very hot – and we came across a swimming area. We had no 'togs'. Someone, with a nod from me, pushed our son Ian (aged 10) fully clothed, into the water. Vic, a dapper little man in immaculate shorts, shirt, long socks and hat, walked to the end of the diving board and spectacularly dived in to join Ian. Soon all were in, shrieking with delight, as we revelled in the cool water. Our young people really knew how to have fun; they really knew, too, how to listen to God and respond to His love. Four of them, two by then married to girls from the Fellowship and two later to marry our girls, felt called to the Ministry. As two had matriculated only in Maths and English – they were qualified technicians – Moore College would not accept them. All four, consequently, went to Ridley College in Melbourne where they did very well in their BD studies.

The Goodna Mental Hospital was in our area and once a month the men visited a ward at night while we women visited our ward, one Tuesday a month leaving at 9 am. I felt these visits could only be worthwhile if they were prayed about. So on the Tuesday before our time, about twelve of us had a hospital prayer meeting at the Rectory. The visiting team were not used to prayer meetings and it took a long time for them to feel able to pray aloud. I would use set prayers or bidding prayers and sometimes they would bring along a prayer to read. Gradually, after a year or so, people began to join in, just talking naturally to God. These were very special times.

I felt surely there should be some sort of after-care hostel for patients such as these. I wrote on these lines to the Minister for Health who replied saying that Queensland had no such hostels and directing me to the Queensland Mental Welfare Association who, he believed, were working to raise money for one.

In June 1963, Dr Noble, the Minister for Health, agreed in principle that an after-care hostel should be bought but explained to the delegation that there were no funds available. At the 1964 annual meeting, Mrs Griffith asked me whether I would take on the Presidency. She said she would give me every support but she was too old to go on. I agreed. Mrs Porter became secretary. This wonderful little group had raised over £4,000 during their years of meeting. Quite a number of the Booval folk, including Col and Dulcie Caldwell, joined the Association. It was decided the meetings should be held in the Rectory. As there was enough money to furnish a hostel, we began to look for a suitable house. We found one in the Ipswich area.

Having found a suitable house, we decided it was time to see the Minister for Health and ask him to buy it for us. I led a deputation to the then Minister, Mr Tooth. We showed him the plans for the house, our financial situation and the details of how we would run the home. He was impressed with the amount of work and careful planning we had done but said, 'There are no funds for this scheme. It would take a miracle for me to buy that house for you.' I replied that I believed in miracles. About six weeks later I had a phone call informing me that the Ipswich house was to be bought at a cost of £7,500 and we were to set it up as the aftercare hostel for patients from Goodna Mental hospital. The miracle had happened. Mr John Herbert, an MP, had spoken up in favour of the allocating of the money.

Now began the really big task of buying furniture and finding staff. We prayed and in response to this, I believe, May and Alan Alcorn, two of our All Saints' parishioners, took up the challenge of being in charge of the hostel. May was a trained nurse and Alan worked in Ipswich. They and their teenage son were prepared to leave their home in Booval and live in the Ipswich house, taking on huge responsibilities, not for financial gain, but for God. Many of the Church members became actively involved in getting the house ready for habitation.

I was privileged to be President at the official opening by the Minister for Health early in 1965. It was a great occasion. The home was called 'Griffith House' in honour of the past President of the Queensland Mental Welfare Association. We felt all the hard work was worth it, for Griffith House was to be a truly Christian home where people could find not only a new life in the world, but also a new life in Christ. The Alcorns were in charge for over 19 years, and even in 1997 Mrs Alcorn relieved every Thursday and slept there on Thursday nights. Col Caldwell, the President who succeeded me, held that office for 13 years. Mrs Porter then took on the job and only relinquished it in 1995, after which she became a Vice-President. It was so good to hear that her work was acknowledged by her being named 1996 Citizen of the Year in Ipswich.

| Mrs Margaret Douglass 2020

My real interest in overseas mission work also began during those years. The Northern Summer School of CMS was held each January at Port Macquarie. We would attend this with quite a number from the parish, en route to Sydney to see Don's family. We bought an enclosed bed-trailer, called 'Storm Bird' officially but which we called 'The Black Hole of Calcutta', a tent and camping equipment. All the family enjoyed our trips south. Camping at Summer School for five or so days, going down to Sydney, and having a few days at the Banana Bowl at Coffs Harbour on the way back made our Sydney trips a proper holiday.

Two couples, Brian and Miriam Chantrill and Bob and Olive Robertson, had gone from Booval to serve as CMS missionaries in North Australia and the responsibility the parish felt to support them was very real. One Thursday, Mrs Porter – a regular worshipper and superintendent of the very large primary Sunday

School at Booval – handed me two dozen eggs and said, 'These must be made up into sponges by tomorrow for the weekly missionary cake stall.' I explained that I had never made a sponge and didn't know how to make one. I was about to add that I had a small baby and life was pretty hectic when I heard, 'Buy a packet of Fielder's Cornflour and follow the recipe on the back'. It was no use arguing. I did as I was told and every Thursday night for the next two years the family had sponge cake and custard for dessert. Every week I made sure I had plenty of eggs in the house so I could produce 2 dozen eggs worth of proper sponges for the missionary stall.

The people in Booval worshipped God with a reverence and awe I had not experienced before. There was never any chatter inside the Church, just a prayerful quiet attitude. In Brisbane Diocese the Sunday morning services were always Holy Communion. I learnt to love and respect this wonderful 'remembrance that Christ died for me' and learnt more and more to 'feed on Him in my heart with thanksgiving'.

During a mid-year trip south to Sydney, Don attended a conference in the St Andrew's Cathedral Chapter House where Agnes Sanford was the speaker. Don came home newly inspired with the reality of Jesus the Healer. He brought back *The Healing Light* by Mrs Sanford so I could read it and join his enthusiasm. The Church certainly was not preaching the power of God to heal in those days. We had experienced that power in a small way in Mt Kuring-gai and later in Booval, when Karen McGrath aged 11 was seriously ill with asthma. Don again called the church to pray and a remarkable healing took place. After that we met regularly to pray for the sick. We didn't advertise a 'Healing Service' in those days. We just did it and we saw God in action. Don felt it should be part of the normal ministry of the Church.

The answer to our prayers was not always physical healing but always there was healing and blessing. One little six-year-old leukemia sufferer for whom we had all been praying, said on the day he died, 'Mummy, I'm tired. I want to go to be with Jesus now.' I was with the family when this happened. They had all come to Jesus through this little fellow's sickness. The funeral was a triumph.

During 1964 we had a Parish Mission. Don invited Bishop Clive Kerle, Bishop of Armidale, to spend a week with us reaching the people with the Gospel. Captain Roy Buckingham of the Church Army conducted a children's mission the week before. The preparation by the people for Bishop Kerle's mission was tremendous. We held a weekly night of prayer – from 6 pm to 6am someone was in the church praying. Except for a couple of hours in the wee small hours of the morning, there were usually quite a number there. We did not pray aloud but just knelt in silent prayer knowing we each were asking God to bless the Mission and to bring people to Himself through Bishop Kerle's preaching. God richly answered our prayers for the meetings and many, not only outsiders, but regular church goers, too, were converted that week. Those prayer times were so special that after the mission a half night of prayer once a month became the parish norm.

When the time came for us to move on to our next parish in 1965, I believe the parish was as sad to lose us as we were to go. We were given a wonderful farewell – generous gifts that have stayed with us into the present. I so value my beautiful blue vase from the Young Wives group and the Noritaki dinner set from the parish. The farewell service was taped for us and we loved hearing the sounds of children's voices, not interrupting, but being part of the service. *'To God be the Glory, great things He has done'*, became our 'theme song' from that time.

5

THE REV JIM STONIER, CURATE
1963-1966
RECOLLECTIONS OF ALL SAINTS' BOOVAL
1959-1966

| Rev Jim and Mrs Diana Stonier

STARTING THE JOURNEY

MY INITIAL CONTACT WITH ALL SAINTS' BOOVAL HAPPENED when I was teaching at Ipswich Boys' Grammar School. I knew parishioners who were members of CMS League of Youth and I had sought Vicar Colin Ware's counsel.

I discovered that a time of great blessing at All Saints' Booval had broken out with the coming of Vicar Colin Ware. This humble godly man had been impressed by CMS missionaries while serving in North Queensland. He promoted Scripture Union Bible reading notes by riding a bicycle around the parish and knocking on doors. Often he sat in the gutter for lunch. A great number of subscribers were enrolled. Once, a man came to the Rectory door for a handout and Colin gave him his second pair of pants off the line. Little did I realize then the significant role All Saints' would play in my future.

A turning point in my spiritual journey had occurred during a weekend visit to Sydney. I heard the gospel through the witness of the Rev Don Begbie in St Paul's Anglican Church, Wahroonga and I was converted. I returned to Brisbane without any church connection.

A friend introduced me to CMS League of Youth. The Rev Jeff Roper and his wife Ursula, had recently arrived in Brisbane as CMS General Secretary and they discipled me. Jeff was a first-rate biblical expositor. A weekly Bible study, CMS League of Youth meetings and occasional camps matured my faith. I also became involved with Scripture Union Bible study notes and S.U. Beach Missions. Being CMS members and being evangelicals in the Anglican Diocese of Brisbane made us unacceptable with some clergy and many members had rough encounters. This strengthened our faith.

I started attending the mid-week Holy Communion service at St Paul's Anglican Church, Ipswich. I did not worship at Booval but, as mentioned above, met many members through League of Youth. Under the Ropers' example and teaching, League of Youth grew and weekend camps exploded numerically, especially after the Billy Graham Crusade. Speakers such as Rev John Chapman and Rev Geoff Fletcher enriched our faith.

CALLED TO FULLTIME MINISTRY

As a counsellor at the Billy Graham Crusade, I witnessed the power of God. Much to my surprise and even more to that of my family and friends, I responded to God's call to fulltime ministry. The Ropers suggested Ridley Theological College Melbourne. I agreed because serving in the Diocese of Melbourne would be good preparation for returning to Brisbane. I supported myself financially for three years at Ridley. Ridley prepared me spiritually and academically for ministry. I was attached to St Jude's Carlton as Catechist, Youth Leader, Sunday School Superintendent and cleaner for three years, earning four dollars a week - a little less than when I was Master-in-Charge of Ipswich Grammar School Prep!

CURACY AT ALL SAINTS' BOOVAL

In my last year at Ridley College I had an interview with Rev Don Douglass, Colin Ware's successor at All Saints'. He asked me to consider a curacy at Booval. We both decided to pray about the appointment. I returned to Melbourne and after much prayer, I wrote saying I felt it was of the Lord. My letter passed Don's letter to me in the post with the same message. I was ordained deacon in February 1963 and priest later that year. My own positive and enriching time at Ridley meant I encouraged parishioners to prepare for ministry at Ridley. Both Don and Margaret were wonderful godly examples. I am godfather to their youngest son, Michael.

Don was a WW2 British War hero, a Red Beret, who jumped at Arnhem and was captured by the Germans after a week of intense fighting. He narrowly escaped being shot when some prisoners escaped. He was a humble godly man with a stammer who, together with Margaret, shaped the spiritual outpouring at All Saints' through their wonderful devotion to Christ. They had previously served with the Bush Church Aid Society at Port Hedland, Western Australia.

Margaret, besides parish ministry, became involved with the Queensland Mental Welfare Association, a group serving patients at Goodna (now Wolston Park) Mental Hospital. Discovering that a cured lady but still needing some care could not be discharged because her husband was in a new relationship, Margaret, as chair of this group, advocated to establish a half-way house for such patients. As a result, Griffith House was acquired and parishioners Alan and May Alcorn volunteered to become full time live-in carers. Margaret Douglass was a real blessing and led many to faith through the women's ministry.

The Parish consisted of six centres - Booval, Bundamba, Dinmore, Riverview, Redbank and Goodna. Every Sunday we celebrated two services at Booval and each of us took services 'down the line'.

Prior to my arrival, the Parish Annual Meeting had decided to suspend all fund raising and concentrate fully on Gospel outreach. All Saints' Booval was mainly a working class parish where wage earners were mostly men who worked at the railway workshop, the woollen mills or in the dangerous, underground coal mines. The parish never had a money surplus but they managed to build a house for me as their first curate, meet their assessment to the Diocese and give substantial amounts to the Church Missionary Society.

I was told the Parish had given little support to their first missionaries, Bob and Olive Robertson serving with CMS in North Australia, until they were convicted of their negligence when the Robertson's little boy, Allan, died of dysentery.

Wednesday night was Bible study and prayer time in the Rectory. On Saturday mornings the League of Youth group of young adults met for an hour in the church for parish and mission focused prayer. A monthly Friday night prayer time was initially devoted to healing. It matured into a monthly half night or full night of prayer in preparation for an evangelistic mission conducted by Bishop Clive Kerle of Armidale Diocese. Parishioners, including the young, volunteered to pray for an hour in All Saints'. I think the all-night of prayer went from 7.30p.m. until 9.30a.m. This continued after the mission and triggered a further blessing of God. I remain a strong advocate for whole nights of prayer as part of my ministry.

I remember visiting a dying lady in Ipswich Hospital, who told me that in a dream she had seen Jesus beside the lake. Being young, ignorant and arrogant, I did not take much notice until Christian members of her family asked what I had done. They told me she had been a difficult lady and had been instantly transformed – even being attested to by the nursing staff. I had done nothing, but God had, in answer to prayer!

My ministry included a day a week at Goodna, teaching RE in

the school and home visiting, building up that centre which, with Redbank, is now part of the Parish of Collingwood Park. The Booval Sunday School grew under the ministry of Mrs Marj Porter and woe betide any teacher who was poorly prepared. GFS and CEBS grew. We bought two go-carts to tear around the church. Our young men built nine two-person wooden canoes under the supervision of Dave Burt, whose daughter Dawn was our female youth leader. We established a Sunday evening coffee shop after church on the veranda of the hall. Dave Burt again helped, building low tables for the youth who sat on cushions. The Friday night youth group, averaging about forty, met again on Sunday nights for Bible study, fellowship tea, worship and coffee ministry. Mens Society, Mothers Union and Young Wives were integral parts of outreach and discipling. Don and I conducted Religious Education at Bremer High. I taught year 12 with each student working through John Stott's *Basic Christianity*. For a contribution of a small monthly amount, members received a discounted Christian book.

A dedicated group of young adults matured in ministry. Here are some of the long-term ripples (All Saints' parishioners highlighted):

Canon Jim Holbeck, Ridley College, Brisbane Diocese, Dean of St Peter's Cathedral, Armidale, succeeded Canon Jim Glennon's healing ministry at St Andrew's Cathedral Sydney, visiting healing ministry in USA. Married **Carole Tapsell** now deceased.

Archdeacon Greg Ezzy, Ridley College, Brisbane & Grafton Dioceses, married **Del Holbeck.**

Rev Tom Wood, Ridley College, Melbourne & Brisbane Dioceses, married **Heather Rasmussen.**

Rev Grahame Stephens, Ridley College, Melbourne & Brisbane Dioceses, married **Sally Saunders.**

Rev Ian McGrath, Moore College, Brisbane Diocese, BCA Brisbane Secretary married to Glenda.

Rev Frank Savage, Moore College, pastoral ministry. A telecom technician debating Jehovah Witnesses turned up to examine what we believed. He was converted and within a few months he could quote large portions of the New Testament from memory. While shaving, he propped Bible Society Bible portions beside the mirror and memorised them. Married to Merle.

Lesley Mc Grath, CMS/SU missionary to Peru. Married Australian SPCK representative Len Woodley.

Dr Alan and Beth Woolard, CMS missionaries, East Africa.

Ivory Shield, CMS missionary North Australia. Married APCM missionary Bruce Shields and served in PNG.

Cyril Neumann (deceased) married **Sharon Cook,** studied at Sydney Missionary and Bible College.

This of course was only the tip of the iceberg. Many of the laity were blessed and became a blessing.

June Singleton, a lifelong friend, made a decision to follow Christ at the 1959 Billy Graham Crusade. She is an L.A. in her parish and leads services in her retirement village especially during COVID lock down.

Graham, an underground electrician, read every atheistic book he could. We talked regularly for about a year. After a meeting at the Bishop Kerle mission, I went through John 3 with him but he could not see it. The next Sunday he walked out of Church and said, "I'm there!" He had been reading John 3 when the Spirit suddenly came upon him. He faithfully served the Lord until his death.

ALL SAINTS' MONTO

With my wife Diana, our six-years ministry at All Saints' Monto was tough, but it taught us spiritually. I had to learn patience in leading country parishioners. Though financially fragile, we prayerfully managed to pay off the new church. Two families became missionaries with Wycliffe Bible Translators and Bryan and Kathy Massey served with CMS. One of our Christian girls married the Scripture Union Children's Missioner.

Our three children were born while we were in Monto. Diana was very ill and desperately needed to be near good medical help. While I was left with our two daughters, Diana had to go to Brisbane for the duration of her third confinement. It was a tough time. Some parishioners were very kind and the Lord looked after us.

THE SOUTHPORT SCHOOL.

Archbishop Felix Arnott appointed me as Chaplain. The Assistant Bishop tried to rescind my appointment but it was of the Lord. I had taught two of the staff. I had studied with one and I knew others. I was readily accepted into the common room. I enjoy teaching. I was Head of Religious Education which, for year 12, became a Board Subject appearing on their Senior Certificate. I also taught Geography, Year 11 and 12 Ancient History and a number of other subjects. Initially I had to do boarding duties during the week and at weekends. As well as teaching fulltime, I was a debating master, convened sport and Airforce Cadets. I led chapel two or three times on Sundays and I celebrated weddings, baptisms and funerals. I spent almost thirty years at the school. Diana and I work as a team seeking to fulfil our wedding text – *Thanks be to God, who in Christ always leads us in triumph, and through us spreads the fragrance of the knowledge of Him everywhere.* 2 Cor 2:14 (RSV).

Living on campus, we were scrutinized 24/7. Boarders often dropped in for food and a chat. We were there to support the students in their successes and griefs. For a number of years we had the whole of year 12 to dinner, including day boys, in groups of seventeen. We stopped when the cohort reached 100.

Each year we lost young "old boys" or students through natural death or accidents. Once we lost three students and a young "old boy" in five weeks. During my time there, we had one murder and a few suicides. Counselling was important. I was made an honorary life member of the Old Boys' Association. We are all like brothers. My ministry continues still, especially in celebrating marriages and baptisms. Parents attended at least three House Services a year. I ministered to many unchurched parents. The voluntary midnight Christmas Service often had three hundred in Chapel and a number outside listening through speakers. "Old boys" would bring their girlfriends.

Diana and I, with the School, sought to reach students with the Gospel through other mediums. We introduced *The St Alban's Art Festival,* an acquisitive, Christian competition. It later became a secular competition open to outsiders. The last insurance valuation of paintings, sculpture and pottery acquired through the *Festival* was $750,000. Before this competition, the walls of classrooms were completely bare even of prints.

By invitation, I was appointed the Inaugural Chair of the Allamanda Hospital IVF Ethics Committee. I held this position for fifteen years. I served on the Board of Emmanuel College, a Christ-centred, strong academic institution, until we shifted to Brisbane. For a number of years we were part of the Scripture Union Coffee Shop ministry in Surfers Paradise. The team, usually about eighty, lived at TSS and Diana served as cook. Each morning I would lead a Bible study.

While the then headmaster and I jogged, we planned a low fee, co-ed, Anglican, Gold Coast school. I 'knew' the name had to be All Saints', after All Saints' Booval and All Saints' Monto. The first block of land we considered was priced at three and a half million dollars. We did not have three and a half cents. Independent of the Diocese, banks were hesitant to lend money for the project. "Nothing is too hard for God"- Gen 18:14. The miracle is All Saints' Anglican School Mudgeeraba, located on a multimillion-dollar campus with an enrolment from K to 12 of about 1800 students. I served briefly on the foundation Council.

CONCLUSION

My three years as curate at Booval in many ways shaped my ministry. I learned the importance of expository preaching together with discovering what God can do when He is sovereign of my life. I learned the importance of regular parish half and full nights of sacrificial prayer as well as the relevance of personally spending an extended time daily with God in Bible study and prayer. I have faced opposition on many occasions but as a disciple of Jesus Christ, I have sought to out-pray, out-live and out-love those who oppose me, but never to out-manoeuvre them.

L to R Jim Holbeck, Carole Tapsell, Grahame Stephens, Del Holbeck, Greg Ezzy, Heather Rasmussen, and Tom Wood

Fun on a Swing Top L to R Ivory Shield, Barbara Barrell, Kathy Mitchell; Lower R Sylvia (Reid) early 1960s

Fun and Games early 1960s Top L to R Greg Ezzy and Richard Naylor, Lower Tom Wood

L to R Kathy Mitchell, Carole Tapsell and Ken Rose at Youth Camp early 1960s

Tom Wood at CMS League of Youth Camp early 1960s

The McGrath family and others at Debra's baptism. (1) Alan Alcorn; (2) Rev Don Douglass with (3) Helen; (4) May Alcorn; (5) Marjorie and (6) Jeff Porter; (7) Margaret Douglass; (8) Jean McGrath (9) Toni McGrath (10) Karen McGrath; (11) Ian McGrath, (12) Jim McGrath, (13) Debra (14) Lesley McGrath

6

LES AND ELAINE VINCENT, BOB AND OLIVE ROBERTSON, AND BRIAN AND MIRIAM CHANTRILL

(ON MISSION IN NORTH AUSTRALIA)

THREE COUPLES WENT OUT FROM ALL SAINTS' BOOVAL IN 1958-1959 to serve in Aboriginal communities in North Australia with the Church Missionary Society.

Les Vincent, a Sunday School Superintendent at Bundamba in the parish, and his wife Elaine, were commissioned at All Saints' Booval on 18 June 1958 to serve at Roper River (Ngukurr). They served in the North until 1962. Bob and Olive Robertson were commissioned at All Saints' on 10 July 1958 for service at Rose River (Numbulwar). Bob was a builder and sawmiller and they served in the North until 1964. Brian and Miriam Chantrill were commissioned at All Saints' on 7 July 1959 to serve at Oenpelli. Brian was a stockman. They served there until 1964.

At the CMS Federal Council meeting in June 1959 *"It was resolved that the greetings of this Council be extended to [All Saints' Booval] Parish who have made such a great contribution to the work amongst Aborigines in the past twelve months."*

Bob and Olive Robertson arrived at Numbulwar with their two children Allan and Ann in September 1958. They were severely tested when their 3½ year old son Allan died from dysentery on Christmas Eve in Darwin Hospital after being flown out that day from Numbulwar. A Memorial Service was held at All Saints' Booval on 26 December 1958. This tragedy triggered a deeper commitment in the parish to support and care for missionaries.

Despite their loss Bob and Olive continued to serve faithfully and on 9 April 1961 they were commissioned at All Saints' for a second term of service at Umbakumba, Groote Eylandt and on 30 May 1962 they were farewelled by the congregation to serve at Roper River (Ngukurr) until 1964.

Each of these couples had been drawn by the Holy Spirit through the ministry and example of the Rev Colin Ware so to know and love Christ that they wanted to share God's love and saving power with the Aboriginal people of North Australia.

Mrs Judith Ware writes in her Recollections:

> "One family's story remains clear to this day: the family of Olive and Bob Robertson. Olive had had some form of Christian upbringing but Bob had had none. After a visit by Colin, Bob responded to his down-to-earth, real, ordinary personality. The Robertsons started coming to church and soon became staunch parishioners. In time they went to the Mission Field (CMS) in the Northern Territory where they started to raise their family. In due course they returned to Booval and continued at All Saints'. Later they moved to Sydney but always retained their faith."

Former CMS Missionary Lance Tremlett reflects:

> "I first met Bob and Olive Robertson at Umbakumba when I went there in 1961. Bob was a saw miller and he worked with teams of Aboriginal men from the community cutting down trees and milling them. Olive worked wherever she was needed. Both he and Olive had quite a sense of

humour. I was single and all the single folk had to eat with the families due to lack of facilities for them. I remember at lunch one day Bob said to Olive, 'The eye doctor said my eyes are perfect.' Olive disappeared and came back with his rifle and said, 'You had better take this back to the doctor. If your eyes are perfect, it must be the rifle that is the problem.'

They were very dedicated to the Lord, great company and good fun to work with. They were very well liked by the Umbakumba people and had a lovely ministry amongst everyone. Bob died some years ago."

In 1972, Ivory Shield and Kathy Mitchell followed in their footsteps. Their stories are included elsewhere in this book.

TWO CHURCHES APPEAL AT ALL SAINTS' BOOVAL IN 1959

The Rev J.B. Montgomery, CMS Secretary for Aborigines, wrote in June 1959:

"Over the past twelve months, three married couples have offered for service in North Australia from the parish of Booval in Queensland, of which the Rev. Colin Ware is the Vicar.......... Early this year the Vicar wrote to ask if there was anything the parish could do of a practical nature to help in the work among Aborigines. He was told of the need for a Church building at the Umbakumba Mission. In due course he replied to say that the Parish would provide the sum of eight hundred pounds by Shrove Tuesday 1960, to enable two small church buildings to be erected, one at Umbakumba and the other at Rose River."[1]

All Saints' Service Register records that in fact one thousand pounds was raised for the Two Churches Appeal by September 1959 in memory of Bob and Olive Robertson's son, Allan Robertson. When the Church of the Holy Spirit at Numbulwar was erected, the Chaplain, the Rev Earl Hughes, wrote: "The building is of stained cypress pine, milled locally and local stone was used for the Chancel and Aisles."[2] A second church, St Mary's Church, was erected at Umbakumba on Groote Eylandt.

The Church of the Holy Spirit, Numbulwar

St Mary's Church, Umbakumba

1. K. Cole: *A History of Numbulwar* (Bendigo Vic.: Keith Cole Publications, 1982) p43
2. K. Cole: Ibid p44

7

JIM HOLBECK

REFLECTIONS ON THE CONTRIBUTION OF ALL SAINTS' BOOVAL TO HIMSELF AND HIS WIFE CAROLE (TAPSELL)

Rev Jim and Mrs Carole Holbeck 2008

ON NEW YEAR'S EVE 1958, WHEN I SURRENDERED MY LIFE to Christ in the flat I was holidaying in, in Boundary Street Coolangatta, I didn't realise that All Saints' Booval would play such a large part in my life in the future.

VICAR WARE

I first met Vicar Colin Ware when I took a brand new convert to Christ to meet him. Bill's conversion as a well-known atheist in

Queensland was a surprise to everyone, especially Bill. He was reading the little New Testament I had given him, when suddenly he staggered out of his room in the Railway Laboratory where we worked. He was ashen faced and shaking like a leaf under the strong conviction of the Holy Spirit. He was saying, *"It's all true isn't it? It is all true. What have I got to do?"* Being only a few weeks into the faith myself, I suggested we go and see this Colin Ware bloke who seemed to be very well respected. He prayed for us both and Bill began to go to his local North Ipswich church (becoming a lay preacher and eventually a member of General Synod), while I decided to attend All Saints' from that time on.

MINISTRY OPPORTUNITIES AT ALL SAINTS' BOOVAL

Ministry opportunities began to beckon and soon I was helping lead CEBS. Later, when Don and Margaret Douglass and their family arrived, I began to help lead Junior church as well. Carole (my future wife) did a lot with the Douglass children and greatly loved and admired the whole family. I was also going to CMS League of Youth meetings in Brisbane and began to lead a branch at All Saints' Booval. This group quickly grew with some outstanding young people joining. One of the younger ones was this lass named Carole Tapsell, the daughter of Eileen, one of the church organists, and of Carl Tapsell, the famous hockey dual Olympic gold medallist who represented India. Carole was the last to be picked up and the first dropped off as I rounded them up for LOY meetings. But as the months wore on, Carole was the last person I dropped off. At the beginning of 1963, I had written these words in my Prayer Diary as I obviously thought about marriage in general, *"Prepare me for her. Prepare her for me. Prepare us for Thee."* I wasn't sure who the "her" was then, but I wanted to be ready for His choice. When I returned home midyear from Ridley Theological College in Melbourne in 1964, it was obvious that Carole Tapsell was the "her" God had prepared for me. Carole and I became engaged just days before my father died of a brain tumour. We married in January 1966 at All Saints' Booval.

| Eileen and Carl Tapsell with Carole

ALL SAINTS' BOOVAL YOUNG PEOPLE IN TRAINING

In 1965, when I was in my second year at Ridley College, Carole and her mother were extremely kind to my widowed mother. Meanwhile it was great to have a Booval contingent with me at College in Melbourne, namely Tom and Heather Wood, my sister Del and Greg Ezzy and also Grahame Stephens who was later to marry Sally Saunders. Kathy Mitchell and Ivory Shield had become nurses and later served in Northern Australia with CMS amongst the indigenous peoples there. Cyril and Sharon Neumann had studied at Croydon Missionary and Bible College and Lesley McGrath served as a CMS missionary in Peru, South America. I believe these close friends of mine have all made a big impact for the kingdom through their ministries over decades.

CAROLE HOLBECK [NEE TAPSELL]

Being such a fun person and already showing signs of becoming a dynamic leader, Carole had a wonderful ministry among the girls of the Booval GFS group. She did well at Teachers College and University and as a Phys Ed teacher in schools in Ipswich and Brisbane. She became a selector and also coach for the Queensland Schoolgirls Hockey team. Carole trained her Brassall High School's relay team. This team broke the state athletic age record. Perhaps thousands of children were taught to swim by Carole at the schools where she taught.

Since her death on 31October 2019 I have often felt like writing reams about what a lovely precious person she was and is and how the Lord had mightily used her during and following her All Saints' days. It is encouraging that a young self-effacing beautiful young girl doing good "stuff" at Booval could later make such a contribution to the church and to the wider world. Following are some quick examples.

1966-68

Ridley Theological College was mainly a men's college in Melbourne. Carole got on well with all the male students and became a hairdresser to some. She had received no training but she did a good free job. As a teacher, she soon won the respect of other Phys Ed teachers in Melbourne and formed deep friendships with fellow staff and students at her Reservoir school.

1969-1972

We returned to Queensland where I was ordained to serve as a curate at St Stephen's Coorparoo. Carol, as a young clergy wife, was involved in many ministries but especially a 20 plus group which met at our home. Our Sarah was born in 1971.

1972-78

When I became the Rector of Mt Gravatt there was a tiny Rectory and no church building. We worked hard to get the parish growing while we cared for Sarah and James who had arrived in 1973. James was born with bent bones and kept falling over his own feet. Callipers were used to enable him to walk more easily. Praise God he fulfilled his dream of representing Australia in seven Rugby Union Tests as a Wallaby! A team effort with very keen parishioners saw Mt Gravatt Parish grow with eventually a new church and later a new Rectory being built and paid for. Carole had a great ministry among the Mothers Union, Womens Guild and especially the lively and exciting Young Wives Dept which she helped build to about 80 young women. Sunday School under her leadership rose from just a trickle to almost the biggest in the diocese.

1978-1988

A new adventure began as I became the Dean of St Peter's Cathedral Armidale. We saw a mighty move of the Holy Spirit there such as we had seen at Booval and so the Cathedral was packed for services. We joined in fellowship with other ministers and the town was touched by our combined outreaches. Carole helped organise a women's luncheon to hear John Smith of the God Squad. This attracted over 800 women with others on a waiting list. Carole, assisted by her mother Eileen Tapsell, also of Booval, had a great ministry among the women and teenagers. Eileen, who had come to live with us, became a much-loved "Gran" (as she was called) to the younger and older generations in Armidale and especially to David, our Armidale addition in 1979.

1988-2006

Our final fulltime ministry was at St Andrew's Cathedral in Sydney where I became the Leader of the Healing Ministry and an Assistant to the Dean. The Healing Service in the Cathedral began in 1960 when a number of people asked Canon Jim Glennon to lead a weekly service at which people could have hands laid on them to receive prayer for healing. It grew to what was described as the largest service of its kind in the Anglican Communion in the world. People came from many denominations to learn how to pray for the sick. I was chosen to continue the service when Canon Glennon retired in 1988.

The ministry expanded at The Healing Ministry Centre [Golden Grove] at Newtown which became a residential centre for people coming to Sydney as well as a place where teaching and prayer ministry could be exercised throughout the week. A team of us would run Cancer Weekends for those with cancer and for their carers. Large numbers of attendees were healed physically and emotionally and many came to Christ over those weekends. Then core-teaching seminars were introduced from Tuesdays to Thursdays where I would teach on the "core" elements of the Healing Ministry in the church. Eventually we had 5 core-teaching stages with 5 or 6 subjects in each stage. We would hold several of these different stages throughout the year. Personal counselling [prayer ministry] was freely offered for guests and for anyone who came to the Centre. We tried to find a need and then to work out programmes based on the word of God to meet that need. I encouraged the members of the Healing Ministry to run other weekly groups at the Centre and some of those were very well attended and richly blessed by the Lord. God alone knows what He did in people's lives in the Healing Service in the Cathedral and at the Healing Ministry Centre, but it was obvious from testimonies that He was mightily at work through both.

Initially, we lived near Beecroft and "Gran" Tapsell moved into the Anglican Retirement Village at Castle Hill where she had a great music and prayer ministry. Carole travelled daily across Sydney to St George TAFE where she became a Head Teacher in Child Studies, a role she loved and for which she won several awards. Later, she became the Senior Head Teacher in Health and Recreation at Loftus TAFE near Sutherland. She built this department into the biggest of its kind in Australia and, as someone suggested, possibly the biggest of its kind in the southern hemisphere. Over the years, she received many awards and one year was a runner-up for the Premier's Award, the top award for all the branches of the Public Service in NSW. She was one of only 22 people nominated from the tens of thousands of people working for the Public Service. At the same time, she ministered at our

Healing Ministry Centre in Newtown and especially cared for staff and guests, many of whom were patients or were visiting patients at the Royal Prince Alfred Hospital nearby.

2006-2019

Carole's retirement function was marked with the biggest attendance that section of TAFE had seen and the head said he marvelled how Carole could mix with, help and integrate all levels of people. Over 80 people attended a special farewell for her in the open, with the same number of dogs, at Sydney Park where she used to walk our dog Geordie. She loved all the dogs, knew all their names and the people from all backgrounds loved her. A great retirement among godly loving believers at Port Macquarie followed until her death in October 2019.

USA MINISTRY

On 10 occasions, Carole and I had the joy of ministering for at least a month at a time in the Episcopal Church in America - in Wisconsin, Alabama and Florida in 1999 and Florida in 2001,2,3,4,5,6,7,8 and 2012. These were teaching missions on healing and we both made ourselves available for counselling prayer ministry during our times there. Over the years, hundreds were ministered to and counselled and Carole loved having more time to minister deeply to people. She, in turn, was deeply loved by the people.

You can see how proud I am of my late beloved Carole but I praise God for all He did in and through her to His glory. I write this also as an encouragement to any young person at All Saints' Booval to realise that when you hand your life over to the Lord, He can do amazing things in and through you.

ADDENDUM

I still have my Prayer Diary for the 1960's and recently found the names of the following for whom I used to pray (for privacy, numbers and not names are given): 22 Junior CEBS, 18 Senior CEBS, 42 League of Youth members, 59 other Booval young people, 19 Junior Church and 28 Booval families.

Praise God for the godly clergy families we were privileged to have at Booval, including Colin and Judith Ware, Don and Margaret Douglass, Jim Stonier, Herb and Marj Robey, Brian Seers, and later Don and Lurline Campbell and others. They all made their wonderful unique contribution to All Saints' and the Kingdom of God.

"To God be the glory. Great things He has done!" - through ordinary folk at All Saints' Booval who were totally committed to Him!

8

IVORY (SHIELD) SHIELDS
MY STORY

| Ivory Shields

DURING MY CHILDHOOD I WAS OFTEN ON THE MOVE BECAUSE my father worked in cement moulding and later in diamond drilling for coalmines and dam construction around Queensland. From our home in Gumdale, Mum and Dad, with their family that grew to three daughters and two sons, spent time in Callide,

Rockhampton, Burdekin River, and Collinsville, sometimes living in tents and huts. Then we came to the Mines Department Camp at Redbank followed by Dinmore. That's how my contact with nearby Booval came about.

I first heard about God and his love at the Gumdale Sunday School while staying with my Grandma. The Bible stories came alive to me as history through RE classes taken by the Rev Brian Whitlock during our time at the Redbank Camp. In my primary school years I attended Beach Mission meetings while holidaying at Hervey Bay and I prayed to God in my heart, though I was afraid of what my parents might say. I came to the assurance of salvation through Jesus when I read John Stott's booklet *Becoming a Christian* and I prayed the commitment prayer that my friend Kathy Mitchell had given me. We were at high school and I was 15 years old.

Greg Ezzy, a friend of ours from a family at the Mines Department Camp, encouraged me to read my bible daily, to use Scripture Union notes, and invited me to teach Sunday School at Riverview. This involved attending weekly classes at All Saints' Booval where the Vicar was the Rev Colin Ware.

Some of the things I remember about Colin Ware are his kind manner of speaking, his dynamic energy and his inspiring leadership of worship. I vividly recall the way he conducted the sacrament of Holy Communion, passionately "pleading the blood of Christ for the forgiveness of our sins". He was always on the move, busy for the Lord. His ministry covered a wide area, with congregations in Booval, Bundamba, Dinmore, Riverview, Redbank and Goodna. He had an extensive Religious Education programme in the schools and he also visited the Goodna Mental Hospital (as it was known then). Colin Ware officiated at my sister's wedding and also prepared me for my confirmation by Archbishop Halse in September 1960. I then had the privilege of teaching in the Sunday School along with Greg Ezzy and Kathy Mitchell.

In 1961 the Rev Don and Mrs Margaret Douglass came to minister at All Saints' Booval. They were a gracious, capable couple, Spirit-led, who loved the Lord, His word and His people. We came to know, love and respect them very much. They had come from Port Hedland, WA, where they had served with the Bush Church Aid Society.

Don sometimes stuttered and could not quite get his words out. That made us listen more attentively and pray all the more for this humble godly man as he preached the gospel. Margaret, his loving wife, was a trained teacher who had adopted their children. I believe that the key to their ministry was prayer. They had a deep sense of reliance on God and His Word and the power of the Holy Spirit. I know that they believed in obeying God's word and sharing the good news of Jesus and all that he has won for mankind, with all people everywhere. They focused on proclaiming the gospel and on God's mission to the world.

We were welcomed into their home on Wednesday nights for a weekly Bible Study. I remember Don teaching from the letter to the Hebrews about "Jesus being a priest forever in the order of Melchizedek - His ministry had no beginning, and no end." We looked up the bible verses, then Don explained it and brought it all together. Visiting speakers also had a deep impact. After hearing a missionary who worked in a caravan hospital restoring sight to the blind through surgery and while also sharing about Jesus, I thought that perhaps nursing was a field in which God might want me to train.

There was a warm and welcoming spirit in the worship services and community life of the church. Young people like me felt loved and accepted. Members of the Mothers Union, Parish Councillors, Lay Readers and their wives, and parents of the young people became friends, opening their hearts and homes to us all. We were surrounded by lovely godly believers. Mrs Eileen Tapsell's hospitality stands out in my memory. I recall attending a Bible Study in her home some years later when Rev Reg Platt spoke on Jesus' words, "My food is to do the will of Him who sent me." (John 4:34 RSV)

Don Douglass was supported by a strong team of lay leaders. These included Alwyn Smith, Alan Alcorn, Alwyn Rose, Jimmy McGrath and Ian Schy. Marjorie Porter, Eileen Tapsell, May Alcorn, Dulcie Caldwell, Joan Schy, Hilda Rasmussen, Doreen

Beadle and Mrs Barrell were just some of the staunch women who worked tirelessly in leadership as well.

Don invited speakers such as the Rev Geoff Fletcher, the Rev Jeff Roper, Deaconess Mary Andrews and missionaries on leave to encourage and challenge us to be more committed in our faith and Christian living. One Sunday morning at Booval, the Rev Ken Short, a former CMS missionary in Tanzania, preached on "the servant girl being sold at the market". He likened the good master to Jesus who bought her, freed her, cleaned her, giving her full status as part of his household. Before this she had nothing. She had no hope, no rights, and was abandoned. Then this wonderful master turned everything around for her. This sermon really impacted me.

We were blessed by having the Rev Jim Stonier as Curate. Once after a meeting, Jim challenged us to get serious about reading books about people who had made an impact on our society and world for God. We bought some of those books to read. I also remember his patient efforts training us to sing a modern version of Psalm 150.

A weekly highlight was the Saturday morning prayer meeting. I greatly valued this opportunity to join with likeminded Christian brothers and sisters in worshiping the Lord and seeking his blessing on our local church and the church worldwide. Jim Holbeck and Tom Wood very kindly collected and brought those of us who had no transport until we had our own motor scooters and could come by ourselves. Besides Jim and Tom, Don Douglass and Jim Stonier, some others who regularly attended that meeting were Carole Tapsell, Heather Rasmussen, Del Holbeck, Greg Ezzy, Grahame Stephens, Sally Saunders, Cyril Neumann, Ken Rose, Joy Henderson, Kathy Mitchell, Mrs Eileen Tapsell and Mrs Marjorie Porter. Earnest believing prayer was indeed the key to all the ministry at All Saints'.

This youth ministry involved not only All Saints' Booval but also League of Youth, the youth arm of the Church Missionary Society. I went on CMS League of Youth Camps at Toowoomba, Alexandra Headlands, Tallebudgera, and Burleigh Heads. CMS purchased a property in the Mount Tamborine Convention

Grounds and set about constructing a hall and accommodation. I had great fun helping at Saturday working bees, driving up from Booval with Jim, Carole, Grahame, Kathy, and my brother Eugene. I am forever grateful to the Rev Jeff Roper, the CMS General Secretary and his wife Ursula for their influence especially in the inspiring Bible studies Jeff gave at League of Youth meetings in their home at Greenslopes and in the city. We also heard reports from students at Deaconess House in Sydney including Margaret Buchan and Ruth Williams. They encouraged us to follow them into further training.

I remember so many things from that time that shaped my future life. I learned that Christianity is about relationships - our relationship with God and living life together with others who share our faith. I learned to trust in God's Word and to submit to Jesus Christ as my Lord and Saviour. I grasped the wonder of God's forgiveness and began to experience the transforming power of the Holy Spirit to make me more like Jesus. I came to realise that, as a disciple following Jesus, I should be willing to go where he leads so that others might have the opportunity to hear the good news of Jesus' death and resurrection, be set free from their guilt and shame and receive new life in Him. I learned that the ultimate goal of anything I might be or do should be to bring honour and glory to God. I was given a firm foundation for my faith and a goal for which to aim. At Sylvia Jeanes' farewell for Sabah in January 1967 Jeff Roper asked me directly, "You're going to be a full member, aren't you?" I said "yes".

MY CHRISTIAN JOURNEY SINCE THEN

I made a commitment for missionary service at a CMS League of Youth Camp at Tallebudgera in 1962 but it would take 10 years of training before I would reach the mission field where God was sending me. I left home at 18 to train as a nurse at the Royal Brisbane Hospital for four years. Nurses Christian Fellowship weekly meetings and 5am Sunday prayer meetings strengthened us for our work and witness in the hospital. This was followed by midwifery training for a year in the Royal Women's Hospital in Melbourne where I resumed contact with Booval friends Greg and Del Ezzy, Tom and Heather Wood and Jim and Carole Holbeck who were studying at Ridley College. I was honoured to have them at my Graduation.

I then returned to Brisbane for Maternal & Child Welfare training in 1968, followed by hospital and community work experience in Brisbane, Ipswich, Goondiwindi and other country towns. I felt God's protecting and guiding hand. Once, after a near miss on the road, I recommitted myself to God and His purposes. I can also remember that after a terrible electric storm, my reading was Isaiah 42:6 - I will send you as a light to the gentiles.

After helping as a nurse at an ISCF camp with Lesley McGrath and where the studies theme was "Jesus is the light of the world", I applied to the Rev Reg Platt, CMS General Secretary, to become a CMS missionary candidate. The first part of missionary training was to study theology during 1970 at Deaconess House in Sydney. My friend Kathy Mitchell and I asked for a training placement with the Rev Don and Mrs Margaret Douglass at St Peter's Cremorne. They were delighted to have us and we were again inspired by their servant hearts. We taught RE in the High School, visited high-rise apartments, attended Sunday services and got to know the parishioners. This was followed by a year at St Andrew's Hall in Melbourne to deepen our understanding of Christian mission and prepare us personally and practically for cross-cultural work. I came to appreciate my dear Dad's efforts in helping me to look after my car. Living in a close community also showed me that I needed to change some of my ways!

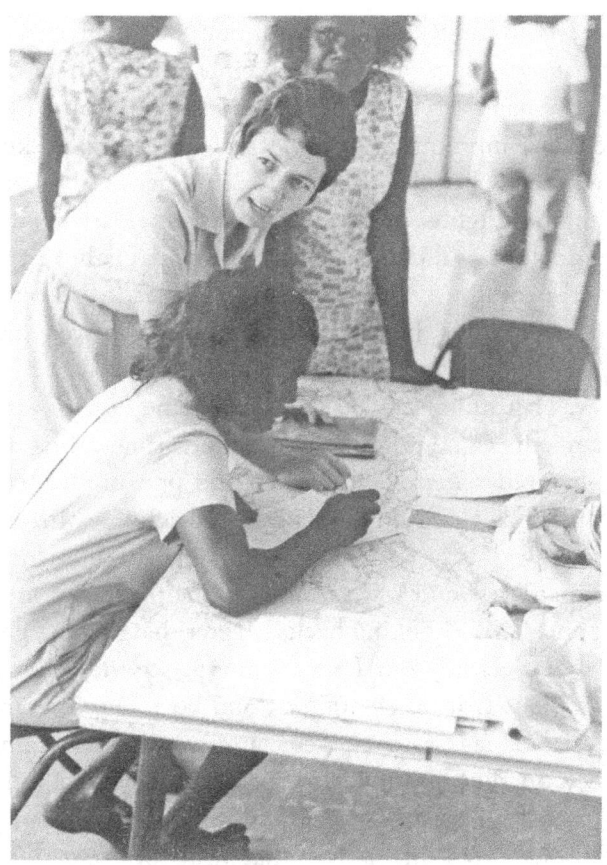

Ivory Shield with Nurses on Groote Eylandt
NT 1970s

I was commissioned as a CMS missionary in All Saints' Booval in January 1972 and immediately flew to Groote Eylandt in the Gulf of Carpentaria where I was based for the next six years. As the aircraft took off from Brisbane my Grandad was heard to say, "Does she know what she's doing?" I joined two other RNs and a team of indigenous nurses training at the Angurugu Hospital - a fifteen-bed hospital consisting of three medical and surgical wards, a labour ward and a baby clinic. We followed directives from the Government's Self Determination Policy, training indigenous health workers as we engaged in community nursing. The aim was "to do ourselves out of a job". There were 750 full-blooded Aborigines in the community and the hospital was a hive of activity. Besides treating surgical and medical emergencies, there was a full range of ante-natal services, plus deliveries, hookworm treatment, leprosy checks, immunizations, checking for ear and skin infections plus radio schedules to a doctor in Darwin about patients, plus arranging flights for serious cases to Darwin or Gove, arranging doctors' and dentists' visits as well as night duty rosters. We were also dealing with sufferers of Machado-Joseph Disease (MJD), a debilitating hereditary disease. After two years I was appointed Sister-in-Charge.

God was faithful and good to us and some nursing sisters and medical students came up to help at various times. This really did help and relieved some of the burden and pressure we felt. There were some difficult cultural and other restrictions with which to cope, and it was easy to become discouraged. I learned many things the hard way and was grateful for the prayers of my friends at Booval and CMS. Looking back, I regret that I didn't give more time to language study but I was happy to see indigenous health workers graduate from their training and be able to communicate in the local language as they were familiar with the community culture. My ongoing passion was that the indigenous folk would come to know and trust the Lord Jesus. That's why I had gone to Angurugu and it was my prayer that my work and my witness would commend the gospel. I had to remember whose I was and to keep my eyes on Jesus.

After six eventful years at Angurugu on Groote Eylandt, four as Sister-in-Charge, I returned to Brisbane and experienced reverse culture shock. I nursed at Ipswich Hospital for two years, was Resident RN at The Southport School for a year and served as a deaconess at Wilston Presbyterian Church for two years.

Then life took a sudden turn. While speaking on a panel at a Missions Meeting at St Andrew's South Brisbane, I met Bruce Shields, a widower with two teenage daughters Robyn and Marilyn. He was speaking at the meeting on the Bible Basis for Mission. Bruce had been an APCM missionary teacher in Papua New Guinea and was continuing to translate the New Testament into the Zimikani and Bagua language back in Queensland from his home at Rosewood. After I had visited Bruce a few times, Robyn and Marilyn said, "She should suit you, Dad!" In due course they were two of my bridesmaids at our wedding on 7th April 1984. That's when my surname changed from "Shield" to "Shields".

After nearly six years at Rosewood, during which our daughter Lauren was born, Bruce completed his translation of the New Testament. Bruce and I followed the Lord's leading to serve in Tari in the Murray Lake region of the Lower Fly River in Papua New Guinea. Bruce had previously served there for some years and knew the people, the culture and the language. From 1990 to 1993, I supported Bruce in his many roles. He was teaching at the Huli Bible School, setting up a ministry training committee, speaking, writing books on teaching and books in simple English and pidgin about the Bible, as well as conducting in-service training for pastors. I had to learn Pidgin and assisted first in hospitality roles, then in nursing after I gained RN registration in PNG. I served in an Asthma Clinic and as a dental nurse. I coordinated optometry and GP appointments, had oversight of missionaries' health, attended to medical emergencies, gave some health lectures and also taught RE in the local primary and high schools.

| Ivory Shields with Tari Tribal Couple in Papua New Guinea

The years since returning from PNG have been full of ministry opportunities. We were part of the pastoral team at Keperra Baptist Church for nearly 10 years, foundation members of North Shore Baptist Church, part of a church plant at Mudjimba on the Sunshine Coast for 5 years and members of the Slavic Evangelical Baptist Church at Coorparoo for three years. Bruce taught for a time at the Mueller School of Ministry at Rothwell and was often called on to lead Bible Studies and teach on Christian mission. I am grateful for the many ministry opportunities I have had through these churches - teaching RE in primary schools, serving as a Girls' Brigade leader for over 5 years, supporting a school chaplain, helping with Mainly Music, visiting aged care facilities, delivering food to needy families, running a coffee shop, sausage sizzles, car washes and bookfests, you name it…!

It wasn't until 2015 that the Zimikani New Testament, which had been Bruce's great passion and achievement, was published and eventually distributed among the Zimikani people in PNG. This was one of the highlights in Bruce's life.

Early in 2016 it was discovered that Bruce had secondary cancers. He felt that he would not have much time left and that his work was finished. He spent precious time with the family and reconnecting with churches where he had served. Eventually he went to be with the Lord in March that year.

Since losing Bruce I have become part of the Carinity Hilltop Gardens community at Kelvin Grove. I sometimes assist in leading the worship services there and engage with the local community through conversational English with overseas students as well as knitting quilts for refugees' children.

God has been guiding me, and I have been very conscious of the prayers of all my friends upholding me. My ongoing passion is to encourage people through my prayers and involvement to come to know Jesus and follow him, to be filled with his Spirit, to serve in his church and to become more like Jesus. I pray that I myself will be obedient to what God shows me through his Word and by His Spirit's leading, through prayer and circumstances, continuing to be involved and active within His church. I believe that our Christian leadership needs to engage with our society, authentically, humbly and with respect; to follow God's leading; to become more like Jesus; to use every technology available and to be salt and light in our society.

This is my prayer for the church:

Oh God of love, come afresh to cleanse and fill our hearts with your Holy Spirit, grace, love and power that we may become more like Jesus, reflecting you; that we may be led by you, through your Word; and with wisdom and truth to accomplish your purposes in your way, in your world, for your honour and glory and the building up of your church, for Jesus sake. Amen.

9

GREG AND DEL (HOLBECK) EZZY
RIPPLES CREATED IN OUR LIVES FLOWING FROM THE RICH MINISTRY AT ALL SAINTS' BOOVAL

Rev Greg and Mrs Del Ezzy

GOD, ARE YOU FOR REAL?

"When I grow up, I'm going to be a missionary," was the prophetic utterance of a very young naïve self to my always caring and encouraging parents who had fostered within me a faith in the God who calls us to serve. They sacrificed so much to give to my siblings and myself every opportunity of which they had been deprived by the fierce depression of the 1930s.

But my first love in my teenage years was sport - soccer, cricket and tennis, interspersed with education, cadetship in Civil Engineering Drafting, girlfriends and religion. Hectic is putting it mildly! But it was a happy, relatively carefree life. Then suddenly came "the spanner in the works" that threw my life into turmoil for some years.

As a schoolboy and later at under-18 level, I represented Queensland in soccer and then captained the Queensland under-21 team. I was flying high and dreaming about a future!

Then, Sunday sport was introduced into our culture followed by my dilemma. Should Christians play sport on Sundays? And if it is ok, what would that mean for my commitment to Sunday worship and teaching Sunday School? The paramount questions for me were, "Is God real and how can I find an answer? Why should I forgo a career in soccer if God is just a belief like believing in Santa Claus?" So, the real and ultimate search for the reality of God began in earnest.

Vicar Ware was my "go to man". He was such a passionate, caring and driven man who had time for young individuals like me. I pummelled him with my questioning every month he turned up at the little daughter church of St. Luke's at Redbank - always at least half an hour late for his fourth service of the morning! I bought myself a Bible. "What version?" the saleslady at the British and Foreign Bible Society in George Street Brisbane asked me. "A little black one please," I replied. I also purchased and poured over *Mere Christianity* by C. S. Lewis.

Then one Sunday morning Vicar Ware picked me up in the parish Austin A40 to take me to his fourth Sunday service of the morning at Goodna where I also sometimes served at the altar in my hot red cassock. Can you believe, that after that service, and now in the middle of a steamy summer day, Vicar Ware drove out into the bush to visit elderly parishioners only to discover that their well needed repairs? So he removed his shirt, and with shovel and mattock strode across the paddock and attended to the problem before returning to the house in a lather of perspiration, to have a cuppa and a sandwich before heading back up the highway to Booval.

That day proved to be the turning point in my search for the reality of God. Vicar Ware declared to me as he drove along that he believed he knew where, at last, I could find my answer. "There's a group called CMS League of Youth who are holding a weekend camp at Shannon Park outside Toowoomba. If you go, I think you will find your answer," he said. Then he organized for me to attend.

He was right! The experience of that weekend enabled me to discern something new about the nature of faith. It provided the environment to begin to live into the practice of faith in Jesus, the Christ. It was for me the beginning of friendships with my contemporaries at Booval where this faith was nurtured through care, worship, Bible study, youth group, service, discussion and prayer.

In those heady days, running late to Evensong meant we stood outside the doors and windows of All Saints' because all the seats would be taken. Vicar and Mrs Ware, followed by Rev Don and Mrs Douglass, were the God-given nurturers of faith in that dynamic young group of God-seekers. These delightful and inspiring people had that capacity of love, humility, spirituality, and leadership that created the crucible for the Spirit to minister. And did I say, that's where I discovered the beautiful lady Deloraine who would become my wife for the next 57 years, but who's counting?

THE RIPPLES ARE CREATED

Following completion of my Diploma in Civil Engineering Drafting, and my transfer to the Mareeba Office of the Irrigation and Water Supply Commission, Del and I were married and our involvement with All Saints' Booval came to an end. However, the seeds of our journey of faith sown in that parish community were starting to blossom. First, the decision to grow that faith with a theological education and later to offer for Ordination, led us to

Ridley College in Melbourne. Curacies at St. Andrew's South Brisbane and St. Luke's Ekibin followed.

Differing communities of faith opened up new opportunities to explore our relationship with God and strategies for ministry. The Rev Bill Carter, Rector of South Brisbane, proved to be a fantastic model of relevant preaching, genuine pastoral care, and mission-oriented marriage preparation for the 300 plus couples married there each year. (How times have changed!) He also set me on a path of strategic planning for effective ministry. He insisted on my participating in a two-year programme of Christian Education and Human Dynamics Training that was instrumental in motivating my further study in Behavioural Science, Leadership and Management, Theology and Counselling. Maybe it's a bit unfair, but I partly blame Bill for coaching me into becoming a workaholic, which habit has taken me a lifetime to break.

Being called to serve with the Bush Church Aid Society, I ministered in the coal and cattle country of Central Queensland for the next 4 years. I established the Parish of Blackwater including the building of the rectory and chapel attached to the house. I was appointed as Industrial Chaplain to the Utah Coal Mine and elected onto Rockhampton Diocesan Council. Philippa was added to our family of Mark and Adrian during that time. It was a very ecumenical ministry with a strong community involvement that included my being the President of the Blackwater Pre-School and Secretary of the lobby group who successfully agitated for a high school to be built. It was an exciting time gathering for worship and nurturing the people of God in a Parish of over 10,000 square miles while establishing regular worship in the aeroplane hangar at a large beef raising property at May Downs over one hundred miles from Blackwater. Up to 100 men, women and children, gathered there for worship and socialization.

Moving to Gladstone, I was commissioned into the role of Regional Director of Industrial Chaplaincy. This involved overseeing the training and managing of chaplains from different Christian denominations as well as negotiating with management and unions to develop industrial chaplaincy in other mines, sugar mills, meat works, engineering firms, retails shops, a tourist island

and an aluminium smelter. The area covered was from Gladstone to Proserpine and west to Moranbah and Peak Downs. This was a unique way of coming alongside workers who never darkened the door of a church.

As Rector of Dalby for 7 years, we were blessed by God to create and develop a large team of lay ministers. Over 150 people participated in the intensive two-year Bethel Bible Study clinics, all led by lay people. At the same time, after-school mid-week ministry with children was established. This enabled Sunday morning worship to be for all ages. As well as our office staff, Grahame and Sally Stephens, other ex-Booval youth group members, joined our team. So we were once again ministering together at a time when attending church was part of the rhythm of life for many more people than it is today. It was a time when the people of God were rediscovering that ministry was for everyone, not just for those who were ordained. The classic words spoken at our farewell have never left me, "He taught us to minister, so maybe we won't need a new Rector!"

During this time, as a member of the Brisbane Diocesan Council, I was asked by Archbishop Grindrod to develop a strategy for the regionalisation of Episcopal Ministry for the Diocese of Brisbane and to steer its implementation through the Synod. This established a much more effective and efficient way in which the leadership could function. Basically, that is still the model being practised today.

After a short ministry at Mt Gravatt, where again team ministry flourished, I became the Rector of Lismore. Various roles in the Diocese of Grafton followed - as Archdeacon and also as acting Administrator of the Diocese for a period of time. During the latter tenure, the hectic days of the Royal Commission into Institutional Response to Child Sexual Abuse required my representing the Diocese at the 10 days of the hearings into historical abuse cases. These related to shameful events some 50 years earlier in the Diocese.

Lismore Parish included ministry at Southern Cross University, the Lismore Parish Pre-School, two large hospitals and the trendy and hippy community of Nimbin. Following a restructure to provide ministry more effectively, parish centres were reduced from six down to a more manageable three. We had a team of five clergy, a Parish Administrator and many lay ministers. One of my talented and passionate curates at that time, Rev Geoff Smith, is now the Archbishop of Adelaide and Primate of the Anglican Church of Australia. Being a regional centre and committed to ministering to people from a variety of expressions of Anglicanism, the ministry team were selected for their readiness to minister with evangelical, liberal, pentecostal, and progressive styles of Anglicanism. Yes, it was challenging but also productive.

After 10 years as Rector at Lismore, I was appointed as a Ministry Development Officer for the Grafton Diocese. I shared in a variety of expressions of this role at different levels over the next 25 years and I continue to be called on today. Currently, I minister on a part time basis in helping the Parish of the Orara Valley to transition to a new twenty-first century way of being the people of God in that place.

I have been associated with Emmanuel Anglican College in Ballina since its creation with sixteen children twenty years ago. It will have an enrolment of over 800 students in 2021 and it has a superb Christian presence and leadership. I continue my involvement there with the chaplaincy team in the role of Chaplain to the staff. After 15 years on College Council, with the portfolio of Mission, I was honoured with the naming of the Ezzy Centre, a multifunctional building for gatherings and food technology. (My grandson, Kristiaan Ezzy, tells his mates that it was named after him as a founding student!)

THE RIPPLES CONTINUE TO FLOW OUT

Reflecting on the ripples still spreading from the work of the Spirit in the life of the community at All Saints' Booval in the middle of the last century, the ministry of Christ continues through the grace of God. Time and time again, His Spirit has bound our family together and enabled us to ride the waves and roll with the punches.

Del's loving spirit and tireless support have been foundational to the ripples continuing. In her own right as well, Del has brought the presence of Christ to the many children she has taught at Ipswich, Melbourne, Blackwater, Benaraby, Dalby, and Brisbane. As Superintendent of the North Coast Children's Home at Lismore she has cared for between twenty and forty severely disadvantaged youth over a period of 10 years. That ministry brought a special citation from the Premier of New South Wales for her work and for her role with the Department of Community Services in developing Government Policies in caring for disadvantaged young people at risk.

Fundamental to the ripples from All Saints' through our lives, has been an ever-deepening awareness of the presence of the Spirit of Jesus progressing our discernment, love and risk taking in the adventurous life of God in us. We are so grateful for the great and mysterious "I AM", as God revealed Himself to Moses. We continue to seek to live as Jesus did, honouring the story of God's people in the Scriptures, while being open to the living Spirit of God who continues to go before us in our time and place.

First it was the rise of Sunday sport that stirred in me the search for God. So too has the realization of the patriarchal history of the church stirred me to discover the equality in which God created male and female, and more recently the scientific acknowledgment of the nature of homosexuality stirred a renewed search of the Scriptural texts that have traditionally informed the negative Christian perspective towards so many grace-filled people, who find themselves orientated to the same sex.

We are so indebted to the foundations that we inherited from the church family at Booval. We will always give thanks for the people of All Saints' and for our colleagues who have been responsible for other ripples from Booval. Especially we give thanks for the loving friendships that God has provided to enrich our journey. With future ripples still expanding, we are confident that God is with us and in us as we pray for discernment and courage to be bearers of the grace of God in the times and places in which we continue to respond in faith.

10

KATHY (MITCHELL) ROBINSON
MY STORY

| Kathy Robinson 2014

I grew up in Riverview, the youngest of five children, on a twenty-six acre farm where Dad grew our vegetables and milked two or three cows morning and night and worked for the Main Roads Department during the day for many years. Mum looked after the family and helped Dad. They were wonderful parents and they always supported me. Dad was a World War 1 soldier and my brother served in the Air Force in World War 2.

I attended Redbank State School and Ipswich State High School. I first met the Rev Colin Ware at St Luke's Anglican Church Redbank where I also attended Sunday School. Vicar Ware came to Redbank School once a week for R.E. and I was in his class. He was always welcome in our home where the door was never locked, as was the custom with so many homes in those days. Vicar Ware would just go in, make a cup of tea, find something to eat and leave a note for us. My Confirmation class of about six was conducted by Vicar Ware on the verandah of our home.

Later I went to the Riverview Anglican Church and became a Sunday School teacher along with Ivory Shield and Greg Ezzy. God had moved in a wonderful way in that Riverview community. This church was made possible by the generosity of my Godmother Mrs Emily Reichardt whose estate was left for the sole purpose of establishing a church at Riverview. With this bequest and the gift of land from the Tessman family and the work of many volunteer men in the Riverview community, a simple church building was established. Mrs Reichardt was fondly known as Aunty Reichardt by many in the Parish including Vicar Ware who used to call her a "prayerful, godly woman and a saint".

Vicar Ware had suggested to my mum that I attend the CMS League of Youth camp being held in Toowoomba in September 1959. So I went! When the bus arrived at Booval I was surprised to see Heather Rasmussen and Del Holbeck, a Prefect and a Senior from High School, getting on the bus to go to Toowoomba. I thought, "This is going to be interesting, having Seniors looking out for me".

It was at that camp that I responded to the invitation to accept Jesus as my Saviour and Lord. Rev Geoff Fletcher was the preacher and Beryl Box was my counsellor. I came home a changed girl. I knew I wanted to serve Jesus and so my journey began. Beryl helped guide me, especially in the early days of my Christian life.

I attended Bible studies on Sunday afternoons at Booval as well as the CMS League of Youth meetings, both in Booval and in

Brisbane, along with various camps at Mt Tamborine, Port Macquarie, Tallebudgera and Alexandra Headland.

During my time in the Booval parish we were expected to serve, and so we did. I went on a few Scripture Union Beach Missions. It was exciting and challenging to be told 'This is what you will do today'. Looking back, I can see I was being trained to serve.

During Rev Douglass' time in Booval I loved attending his Wednesday night studies at the Rectory. One night I wore a brightly coloured shirt and Rev. Douglass said, "When I am Archbishop I will have my mitre in that colour." He liked a joke and was easy to talk to. During our time at Deaconess House in Sydney, Ivory and I worked in the church where he was the Rector. He and Margaret encouraged us to grow and follow God's leading.

As I always wanted to be a nurse, I commenced four years of training at the Royal Brisbane Hospital in January 1962. This was followed by a year of midwifery in Melbourne and 6 months of infant and child welfare training in Brisbane. During this time I met missionary nurses and the possibility of my becoming one deepened. Thus I proceeded to gain experience in many fields of nursing. In 1970 I went to Deaconess House in Sydney for theological training and after being accepted by CMS for missionary service, I went to St Andrew's Hall, the CMS missionary training college in Melbourne in 1971.

There were so many at Booval who influenced my life, such as Jim and Carole Holbeck, Tom and Heather Wood, Del and Greg Ezzy and Jim Stonier. I especially remember Alwyn Rose and Alwyn Smith conducting Evensong at the Riverview church. So many wonderful Christians at All Saints' encouraged me, prayed for me, and supported me when I went to Oenpelli in 1972. The friendships I formed with many of them have lasted to this day.

The CMS General Secretary, Rev Jeff Roper and his wife Ursula taught us how to live the Christian life and opened up the wide world of Christian mission. I remember arriving at a camp one Friday evening as a hut 2 I/C and being encouraged by Ursula to be proactive, to take an interest in everyone, and particularly to get to know the eight girls in my hut by their names.

On the same night in January 1972, Ivory Shield and I were commissioned as CMS missionaries at All Saints' Booval by the Rev Reg Platt, CMS General Secretary, and the Rector, the Rev Herb Robey. I was appointed to go to Oenpelli (Gunbalanya) and Ivory to Groote Eylandt in the Northern Territory.

My life was about to change again. I was asked to help the nurse at Rose River for a few weeks before going to Oenpelli. The pilot of the plane that came to get me was Ted Robinson, the man who was to become my husband. In January 1973 we were married back in All Saints' Booval where I had been commissioned to serve in Oenpelli twelve months previously.

Kathy and Ted Robinson with Melanie
Northern Territory 1970's

Ted and I continued to serve at Oenpelli for almost 5 years, Ted as a pilot and I as a nurse. During that time we saw Oenpelli transition from a mission settlement to an autonomous community. I loved nursing at Oenpelli and though there were challenges and disappointments I learnt to look to God for His help. I remember one night waiting for dawn to come so that the aerial medical plane could land and evacuate a child who had been poisoned by a snake bite.

In 1976, MAF (Missionary Aviation Fellowship) assumed responsibility for the CMS plane and in December that year we moved to Perth with our first two children. Eventually our family grew to five children, all of whom are married and our tenth grandchild is due in 2021.

Our Christian walk has seen many changes. Currently we attend the Christian City Church in Perth. We have maintained contact with the CMS Branch in Brisbane and now with the Perth Branch. I find it exciting to see the different people God is calling and the places where they are going to serve.

I sometimes wonder how I had the courage to go and serve in the Northern Territory, but then I remember that God does the calling, the preparing and the training. "He calls and leads - we listen and follow."

I see a mission field right here in Australia. There are so many people from different lands and faiths who need to know about Jesus. I pray I will always be ready to witness in His strength and by the power of His Holy Spirit.

I have been blessed by opportunities to lead and assist in ladies' bible study groups. For ten years I was part of a team visiting an aged care facility. We conducted services for special occasions such as Christmas and Easter as well as Anzac Day and Remembrance Day. I love being with the elderly and continue to work in Aged Care in a Resident Liaison role.

I look forward to the future knowing that God is in control. Our circumstances may change but He never changes. I will always be thankful for my early years at All Saints' Booval. I pray that, in the words I remember learning from the Baptism Service so long ago, that I "may continue Christ's faithful soldier and servant unto my life's end." (*1662 Book of Common Prayer*)

11

GRAHAME AND SALLY (SAUNDERS) STEPHENS

ALL SAINTS' BOOVAL MEMORIES

Rev Grahame and Mrs Sally Stephens with Jonathan

IF I CLOSE MY EYES LONG ENOUGH, TIME ROLLS BACK SOME 60 years and I'm sitting on a wooden pew on a summer day in All Saints' Booval and we're having our weekly prayer meeting as we did every Saturday morning. I recall we were praying for people to come to Christ and as we took turns, Tom Wood jumped in and said, "We need to put a bomb under people!" Well, I didn't know it then, but as it turned out God answered that prayer, and he did just that. The twist was, he put the bomb under us!

My time at All Saints' Booval was one of the most formative experiences of my life. Although over the course of a lifetime it was relatively short, 1960 - 1965, there's no doubt my time there set me on the path to become a minister as it did for so many of us [Jim Holbeck, Greg Ezzy, Tom Wood]. I met and married my wife Sally Saunders there and built some wonderful friendships with the likes of Jim Holbeck, Carole Tapsell and others.

I joined the parish as a newly minted Christian right after the Billy Graham Crusade in 1959. I was in my early 20's and on fire for the Lord. I was invited there by my nephew Ken Rose, the son of church members Alwyn and Millicent Rose. He invited me to a League of Youth meeting and before I knew it, my whole life revolved around church. We would go to League of Youth, Sunday School, prayer meetings, bible study and eventually Parish Council - and of course Sunday services - morning and night! It was a special time of fellowship with God's hand clearly on us.

We were blessed by the faithful and biblical ministry of Rev Don Douglass and Rev Jim Stonier. They would preach on Sundays to over a 100 of us. Our youth ministry was bursting at the seams with 125 members and I recall we had one of the largest Sunday Schools in the state.

I have many fond memories of my time there. One that always makes me smile is that just before Christmas, maybe a week or so beforehand, we'd borrow a car (Peter Moody's from memory), slap a speaker on it, and Jim Stonier and I would drive around bellowing out the Christmas service times and encouraging people to come. How times have changed!

Eventually I left to attend Ridley College in Melbourne. I graduated from Ridley in 1968 and so began my own ministry. Having married Sally in that same year, we started our lives together in our first parish of Greensborough, Victoria.

Again God blessed us. As a curate I had excellent teaching, leadership, and hospitality shown by the resident parish priest Rev Charlie Maling, and his wife Mary.

Sally and I were also excited to begin our family with the

arrival of Jonathan, our only boy and the first of 4 children.

After a busy 3 years there, we continued to move around spending time in Winchelsea and Springvale over what would turn out to be roughly 10 years of ministry in Victoria. By that time we had 4 children under the age of 6 with the additions of Rebecca, Sarah and Jennifer. While we loved our time in Victoria, we were keen to return to Queensland and seek the support of family with our four energetic children!

God heard our prayers and we packed up and moved to the lovely country town of Dalby in Queensland where we reunited with fellow one-time Booval members Greg and Del Ezzy. We both ministered at St John's Anglican Church Dalby. It was lovely to meet new friends there and it also allowed us to make regular trips to Booval to connect with family.

Finally we made our last move to Brisbane where Sally and I had the privilege of serving at St John's Anglican Church Wishart for over 20 years before retiring in 2000. During my ministry time, we had the usual ups and downs that life always brings, but with each circumstance, it only reaffirmed our faith in God as sovereign in all things - a truth that we learned all those years ago as young Christians worshipping in the pews of Booval Anglican Church.

However, my ministry wasn't quite over. I had the privilege of becoming General Manager of the Queensland arm of Samaritans Purse - the charity founded by Billy Graham's son Franklin. After decades of serving in the church, it was an unexpected and joyous opportunity to serve God in such a different way - worrying about the daily logistics of getting shoe boxes filled with Christmas gifts and delivered to those in need in foreign countries. I still remember the joy of handing over my first shoebox to a young child on a trip to Cambodia and seeing them experience something of God's love.

It also seemed a fitting end to a wonderful time in the ministry that had its seed planted and nurtured 60 years ago at Booval. All Saints' Booval is a fine parish and I feel privileged to have been a part of it. Fondest regards to All Saints' Booval from Grahame and Sally Stephens.

12

LESLEY (MCGRATH) WOODLEY
MEMORIES OF ALL SAINT'S BOOVAL

| Lesley McGrath

I AM ONE OF THE POST WW2 BABY BOOMERS GENERATION, the eldest daughter of Jim and Jean McGrath and I am grateful to God that All Saints' Booval was our family church. The Rev Colin and Judith Ware and the Rev Don and Margaret Douglass were significant people in my coming to faith in Jesus as my Lord and Saviour and in my growing commitment to Christian mission.

Under Colin's oversight we had a huge Sunday School at All Saints' with over 400 children. I was sent every Sunday and remember, at the age of eight, reading a missionary biography (probably a Sunday School prize) and promising God that I would serve him in South America. Though at the time I felt that I would never be 'good enough' for that, the seed was planted. That same year I was enrolled in the GFS, led by Hilda Rasmussen.

At the age of 12, I was prepared for Confirmation by Colin Ware. He instructed us in the Catechism, the Creed, the Ten Commandments, the Lord's Prayer and the Sacraments. I was dressed in white with white gloves and veil and presented to the Archbishop along with about fifty others. I knew this was a significant time but understood only a little. I was growing incrementally in faith. God was at work in my life.

The Billy Graham Crusade in 1959 resulted in an influx of young people a few years older than me, into All Saints'. They organised a youth group and took me on my first youth camp at Shannon Park just outside Toowoomba in November 1960. There I learnt two Bible verses... *Romans 3:23 (RSV)...For all have sinned and fall short of the glory of God...* and *Romans 6:23 (RSV)...The wages of sin is death but the free gift of God is eternal life in Jesus Christ our Lord.* That set me searching. By this time I was in a post-Confirmation bible study group led by the minister's wife, Mrs Margaret Douglass, in her home.

In mid 1962, I asked the Rev Don Douglass, "What do the leaders of our Youth Group have but I don't?" He talked about Jesus but I still didn't understand. However, it became clear at the next youth camp at Mt Tamborine in November. It was there that I submitted to Jesus as Lord, wanting to follow Him with my whole life. I began to read my Bible and pray. Little did I realise the impact this would have on my life. Early each Saturday morning at the church, keen youth leaders joined to pray for missionaries. I joined them and learnt much as I listened to their earnest prayers for both our Youth Group and those serving in distant places. I gained a grounding in prayer and missionary awareness.

Understanding that my relationship with God meant

following Jesus, I had a strong desire to see my friends come to know Jesus as well. I read books like *Purpose in Prayer* and prayed for opportunities to speak of Jesus, particularly with friends at school! Many friends responded and came to our Youth Group.

I loved going to camps and was always on the lookout to find a way to earn money so I could attend more. In 1963 the local lawnmower shop ran a promotion – pushing a lawn mower – a race from Ipswich Central, up Limestone Hill to Booval (about 3 kilometres). Being young and female, I was chosen by the local paper at the start line for a photo! I lined up with the others not knowing what to expect. I ran hard and reached the finishing line exhausted but to find I had won the prize for the women's section. The prize was enough to cover the fees for the next two camps!

In the same year I was excited to be asked to teach a class on my own in the 'big' Sunday School. I had been teaching a group of pre-schoolers for a couple of years but now had a chance to teach 8 year olds. I also led the singing for the whole Sunday School. One of the favourite songs was *Draw your swords, Use your Swords, for the Battle is the Lord's!* To illustrate, I took along my Grandfather's bayonet from the 1st World War, brandishing it high as we sang. My prayer life was growing as I learnt to bring my concerns to my Heavenly Father.

I began to keep a personal diary. On Easter Day 1963 I wrote, 'I wish more people knew Jesus. When I am old enough I am going to Deaconess House in Sydney to prepare myself.' Later that year I was asked to speak at the Youth Club and relished the opportunity. Afterwards I wrote: 'Thank you for the help and guidance You gave me to speak at the Youth Club.'

1963 was also the year of my first League of Youth (CMS) camp. It was in August and was held for teenagers at the Mt Tamborine CMS campsite. My group leader was Fay Cutmore. She had her work cut out as we younger people got up to all kinds of innocent pranks like short sheeting her bed. She pretended not to notice our midnight feasts. She took it all in good humour and I grew to respect her.

On the 1964 Anzac Day weekend, I led a Booval GFS Camp at Tamborine. My knowledge of the Bible and mission grew steadily as we engaged in discussion and study. In September I wrote: 'I pray the LORD will guide me. Help me to work hard and to do well in my Junior and Senior exams.' and again in October, 'Not long now till my Junior exams. Please help me to remember what I study, Lord.' I worked diligently wanting to do well.

I am grateful to Don and Margaret Douglass for introducing me to Scripture Union. They took me to an Inter School Christian Fellowship (ISCF) leadership camp in 1964. This was my first Scripture Union experience and became a major turning point in my life. I discovered not all Christians who committed to Jesus as Lord and read their Bibles and prayed as I did were Anglicans! Relationships begun at this camp continue today. The theme hymn became my prayer... *Let me burn out for Thee dear Lord, burn and wear out for Thee. Don't let me rust or my life be a failure my God to Thee. Use me and all I have dear Lord, and get me so close to Thee, that I feel the throb of the great heart of God until I burn out for Thee.*

I returned from camp to Year 11 enthused and wanting to start an ISCF group at our School. Somehow I found a teacher who was a Christian and asked her to help me. We gathered a small group together and met weekly to sing, pray, and listen to speakers. A few times, I gave the talk and was surprised at how members of the group listened and were helped.

I loved the experience of camps - the fun, the learning, and the beauty of the creation in the bushland settings of Tamborine Mountain. So I went whenever I could. This laid a foundation for my future ministry in camping. I did not see it then, but understood later, how God was guiding my life experiences. Just after the 1965 ISCF Leadership camp, I prayed "As I look to the future, Father, I give myself to YOU for your use. I want to continue to grow in faith and to learn to pray with thanksgiving."

CMS Summer School became an annual event for me. My family attended for the next two years. Then my friends Jim and Carole Holbeck took me in 1966 and I went every year after that until I went to Peru.

For a long time teaching had been on my horizon. I worked

out that after finishing Year 12, I would head to Teachers College to do the two years of training, fulfil the two-years bond, then head to whatever preparation was needed to go as a missionary to South America as a teacher. These were my plans. God's ways were infinitely better.

Even while studying for my Senior exams, I found time to attend preparation meetings for my first Beach Mission at Shorncliffe in the summer of 1965-66 – from Boxing Day to New Year's Day. I began to understand the breadth of the Scripture Union ministry. Beach Mission was a labour-intensive time of daily building sand pulpits, gathering children and using whatever means possible to introduce the children, young people and their families to Jesus.

I expected to matriculate with sufficient marks to achieve a scholarship to Teachers College. But I didn't! I was able to sit for a supplementary in Maths 2 which I passed. I had only one more subject to do to get into Teacher's College. The Curate, Jim Stonier, who lived next door to us, told me to get my attitude right and trust God to know what He was doing. He suggested I get a job and study at night school. I found a position in the Queensland University library. This enabled me to study French and Ancient History at night school in order to improve my matriculation score. I also learnt a lot about books and I could see God's hand in this.

Active involvement in All Saints' Booval, my home church, was a given. I was the junior leader of the GFS group. Many in the group were only two or three years younger than I was. I was greatly encouraged when one of the girls, Beth, made a decisive commitment to Jesus.

As soon as I went to Teachers College, I joined the Teachers College Christian Fellowship (T.C.C.F) and revelled in the fellowship and Bible studies. We had several camps where we got to know one another well and where my mother Jean volunteered to be the camp cook. I can see now that her way of showing her love was by doing. I am surprised to realise I am more like her than I had thought! In 1968, I started the Physical Education first year studies at the University of Queensland while doing second year at Kelvin Grove Teachers College.

All Saints' Booval continued to supportively follow my progress as I taught physical education in Ipswich then in Townsville. In each school I was able to initiate ISCF and to create innovative teaching plans that enabled even the least athletic students to participate with enjoyment and a sense of achievement.

I was convinced that God's plan for me was to leave teaching and go to Deaconess House in Sydney, followed by study at St Andrew's Hall – the Melbourne based CMS training college. In due course I became a CMS missionary and was seconded to Scripture Union (Union Biblica) Peru. Looking back, I can see how every experience of my life to that point had equipped me for the ministry opportunities that unfolded during the six years I served in Latin America and I rejoice to hear how God's grace continues to bear fruit in Peru.

Back in Australia I have been privileged to serve our Lord in a number of roles, as a bookseller at Ridley College and Education Officer at CMS Victoria. Since my marriage to Len Woodley in 1989, I have worked in administrative roles with Scripture Union and CMS in South Australia and with CMS National Office and SparkLit (SPCK-Australia).

I am so thankful for the spiritual foundations that were laid in my life at All Saints' Booval. To God be the glory!

13

TOM AND HEATHER (RASMUSSEN) WOOD

LIBERATED BY GOD'S LOVE

Rev Tom and Mrs Heather Wood 2016

TOM'S STORY – SAVED TO SERVE

AT THE END OF 1958, AS A SEVENTEEN-YEAR-OLD BODGIE and a fan of Elvis Presley, I was searching for meaning and direction in my life. I had been reading books that were trashy and all about sex when a librarian in Ipswich suggested I read Lloyd Douglas' novel *The Robe* about a Roman tribune and his Greek slave who became followers of Jesus after they encountered the seamless robe taken from Jesus at his crucifixion. I could barely read it. The words were too big but I wanted something different. So on holidays at Brunswick Heads, I was reading *The Robe* in my bedroom when I had a deep spiritual experience. It was a very personal encounter of the tangible and overwhelming presence of God. I didn't understand it and I was scared that I might be going insane. However, I thought I would go to church the next Sunday. Standing outside the Anglican Church at Brunswick Heads, I noted every man going into that church wore suits and the women wore hats. Not for me! I only had my bodgie pink shirt and iridescent green-flecked jacket!

Back home, the curate of St Paul's Ipswich suggested I contact Rev Colin Ware at All Saints' Booval "who understands that kind of stuff". Colin responded, "If it was real, Tom, you will still be with us in three months time." He was right. It must have been real because that was 62 years ago.

I will never forget my first Sunday at the 7.15am service in All Saints' Booval. The usher handed me a 1662 Prayer Book. I opened it at page 1. I couldn't find a thing. The ritual of the service meant nothing to me but I kept going to church, drawn by Colin's passion and sincerity. He always preached in the pulpit below a cross carrying the crucified Christ. I loved his preaching that was always centred on Christ. And there, at his feet as it were, I began to grow and to understand what it meant to be a follower of Christ.

In 1959, I attended a Billy Graham Crusade meeting at the Brisbane Showgrounds and I went forward at the invitation time, but it didn't "click" for me then. A few months later, Colin encouraged me to go to a CMS League of Youth Camp at Alexandra Headlands. It was there I truly encountered Jesus as my Saviour under the ministry of Rev Geoff Fletcher and Rev Jeff Roper.

My life then became centred on Christ but I was still a young man struggling with a lot of issues. It was primarily Colin who gave me the support I needed. I was in my second year of a five-year apprenticeship in Radio and TV and I often called in at All Saints' after work to spend time in prayer. The church was always open and every week I would spend time with Colin who always welcomed me. He modelled to me what Christ was like. His life forced me to read and search the scriptures. And besides I had a lot of fun doing it.

My own father and mother were not churchgoers. Both my grandfathers were active communists. My mother affirmed my new faith and would occasionally come to church. My father kept his distance, although in latter years, I had the privilege of leading him to Christ and he became my best friend. Colin was always straight and to the point. He was a father figure to me as well as a shepherd. I never doubted his sincerity or his deep care. I realize now he also kept a distance between us to allow the Holy Spirit to work in my life. Later, I found out that Colin led my mother's mother (now living in the parish with her second husband at Dinmore) to Christ when he was at Mossman in North Queensland.

Colin had served in the Brotherhood within the Anglican Church and had taken a vow not to marry for 10 years. Thus he was in his forties when he married Judith early in his ministry at Booval and where two of their five children were born. Judith was a gracious wife and support to Colin. Both were wonderful parental examples.

Colin visited homes in the parish mostly by foot or by bicycle. He would always wear his black shirt with the identifying crosses on the collar. This was not a status symbol for him, but helped people to acknowledge his unique role in the community. His passion was to share the Gospel and have the Bible read in every home. He appointed me as Scripture Union secretary and he would tell me which families to follow up from his visits. I used to leave Daily Bread and other notes from Scripture Union with folk and encourage them to read the Scriptures meaningfully. This impacted me too, so that the Scriptures became central in my life and many of these people became close friends.

Eileen Tapsell was a gentle and godly lady, who, with her husband Carl and daughter Carole, migrated from India in the late forties. Eileen asked me to pray for Carole and I remember when she committed her life to Christ as her Lord. I also recall Arthur and Hilda Rasmussen, Jim and Jean McGrath, Alwyn and

Millicent Rose, Alan and May Alcorn, Alwyn and Del Smith and the Schluter & Schy families plus Allan Wallis, Johnny Porter and Cyril Neumann (later to go to Sydney Missionary & Bible College). In 1964, Jim Holbeck (later to marry Carole) and Greg Ezzy, married to Del Holbeck, went to Ridley College. In 1965, Grahame Stephens (later to marry Sally Saunders) and myself now married to Heather Rasmussen, joined them there. Kathy Mitchell and Ivory Shield went as CMS missionaries to North Queensland after their nursing training. After all these years I still feel close to my mate Ken Rose who was killed in a road accident in 1965. These were friendships I greatly valued plus many more that positively impacted my life.

Others whose love, guidance, example and teaching I recall with gratitude include Rev Jeff and Ursula Roper, Secretary of CMS and League of Youth. Every Christmas holidays I went to Scarborough Beach Mission and worked with children. There, I met Pa and Ma Kilvert who, together with Colin Ware, made the biggest impact in my life at that time. I also acknowledge the part All Saints' Sunday School played in my spiritual growth and developing ministry. Mrs Marjorie Porter, the Superintendent, always 'shot from the hip'. Very early on, she "button-holed" me to teach Sunday School. Looking back, I think it was a case of the blind leading the blind, but my heart was right in it for Jesus and I learnt a lot.

I'll never forget the day Colin told me he was leaving All Saints' to become Rector of St Stephen's Newtown in Sydney. I was devastated. He had become like a father to me. I wept. A sense of aloneness swept over me. Heather and I spent time in our little wooden church praying our way through our grief. We were given Philippians 2:12 (RSV) "...work out your own salvation with fear and trembling". What I didn't know at the time was that the couple who would take Colin and Judith's place would usher in another chapter in my life.

The Rev Don Douglass and his wife Margaret, originally from Sydney, had served in Port Hedland with BCA before coming to Booval with their three small children. I vividly remember their deep and abiding love for God our Father. Don always affirmed this love when he preached and when he shared personally with me. Don and Colin came from very different backgrounds, but they both loved God and served Christ. I can recall sitting in church listening to Don preach. He stuttered. He would tell us about the "l-l-l-love of G-G-G-God". I think all of us young folks were saying the words with and for him. However, one couldn't deny his love for God as he showered it upon us and as he lived and spoke. Margaret, his wife, became heavily involved in parish life, particularly in establishing a Young Wives group. She also spearheaded a work in Mental Health with the inmates and those being re-established into the community from the local Wolston Park Hospital. Both Don and Margaret were a real joy to be around. Don modeled to me how to be a loving husband and a great dad.

In 1963, Rev Jim Stonier was appointed as our Curate. Jim embraced life and lived for Christ in a positive and joyful way and as youth leader became a strong influence in my life. He showed me what following Christ was all about. His ministry freed Don to get on with building up the parish community.

Towards the end of 1963 Heather had decided to go to Sydney Missionary and Bible College in Croydon. We had become engaged in the previous June. She had been accepted to start in 1964. For some time I had been toying with the idea of going to Ridley Theological College to be trained for lay ministry. I was not considering ordained ministry at all. To gain entry to the College, I needed to complete further studies which I did part time at night. The final examination results were not released until late January 1964, too late to enroll for that year. In late December, Heather challenged me to consider going into Bible College with her. I raised many objections including that I didn't have enough money to do so, but God had other plans. During a day of prayer and fasting, each objection God countered with Scripture verses such as, "You who have no money, come, buy and eat." (Isaiah 55:1 RSV) and finally, "Have not I commanded thee? Be strong and of a good courage." (Joshua 1:9 RSV) I finally yielded to God. So I resigned my job as a qualified TV Radio Technician.

My year at SMBC increased my love for the Bible even more

while expanding my knowledge of mission and missionary work. I learnt to rely on God particularly in uncomfortable and challenging situations. But this time also allowed us both to reconnect with Colin and Judith Ware at St Stephen's Newtown. Colin had us walking the streets of Newtown. I will never forget one Sunday afternoon. Colin told me to bring my piano accordion and to follow him. We ended up in a park in Georgina Street. Colin stood up on a picnic table and began to preach. Up shot the windows of the tenement houses as people gawked and listened. I was wishing the ground would open up and swallow me. When he finished, he pointed at me and said, "Play!" With my fingers jumping around with nervous tension I pushed out the tune as we sang, "I will make you fishers of men". When I finished playing, I looked up to see a wall of kids running down the road and into the park towards us. As they surrounded us we told them a Bible story. From then onwards, every Sunday Heather and I would conduct open air Sunday School in Georgina Street park using our Sunday School flannel graph material that Heather had made through Child Evangelism Fellowship. We were invited into some homes for coffee - Continental style - strong and black. As opportunity arose, we shared the Four Spiritual Laws of the Gospel. Each week, the children would line up and listen as we told them Bible stories. They loved it and we loved them. We later heard that this Sunday school continued for nearly twenty years.

HEATHER'S STORY – CLAIMING THE PRIZE

> Matt 13:45-46 - From a grain of sand to a pearl of great value!

In 1956 a thirteen-year-old girl knelt beside her bed and cried out to Jesus how much she needed Him and wanted Him.

It was quite early in Rev Colin Ware's ministry and I had just come home from Evensong as a regular attendee, always drawn by some magnet to have to be there each week. That night, Colin preached on Matt.13:45-46 about the pearl of great price. He spoke about the Thursday Island pearl divers who were constantly hoping to find great treasure - an exquisite pearl exceeding all other pearls they had found before. As he spoke, I knew that I desired Jesus, THE Pearl of Great Price, more than anything else I had ever wanted. What's more I knew I needed Him to face my life and my future. I needed help to overcome pent up anger from childhood hurts and wounds. I didn't understand the significance of that step at the time. I didn't know that that night the angels in heaven were rejoicing over me. But that night began a pilgrimage, the start of my journey with Jesus in the Kingdom of God. I told no one. It was my private decision; but from then on I began to search the Scriptures. I found an inner strength I had not had before to be able to say "no" to situations that had crippled most of my childhood.

I was baptised at All Saints' as a baby and I remember how the curates (later to be Bush Brothers) on staff at St Paul's Ipswich radiated the love of Christ when they visited our home. I loved the fellowship and fun activities in the GFS (Girls' Friendly Society) of which my mother, Hilda Rasmussen, was a leader. Although I sometimes mucked up in classes, I still won yearly Sunday School attendance prizes. I have vivid, happy memories of the special train stopping at all stations from Ipswich to Goodna, collecting children and their families for the fabulous combined Sunday School picnic at Sandgate.

Mrs Hilda Rasmussen GFS Leader All Saints' Booval 1950s and 1960s

However, at home within the extended family, I was facing situations that I couldn't handle as a child. I felt I was to blame and anger began to build up in me against my world and just about everyone in it. When Colin Ware came to Booval Parish in 1955, I immediately saw the love of Christ in him and I longed to find out more. In his early months at Booval, Colin married Judith and together they settled into ministry as well as starting their own family. I was honoured to share some of their family moments as I babysat for them. Much to the delight of a young teenager, they took me on one of their holidays to Uralla where I shared the simplicity of their lifestyle in a "vicarage swap". Judith's quiet and calm demeanour taught me much about the grace of God working in a life given in service to God and to others. I remember being with Judith at a church service at a camp or day apart when she modelled quiet devotion as she gently reached out and told me to kneel.

Colin's passion for Christ also shone out in his walking and riding his bicycle around the streets of the Parish, greeting the locals, getting to know them, visiting them in their homes, introducing them to home Bible reading through Scripture Union and eventually leading many to Christ Himself. The Parish became alive with the Spirit of God.

I recall now with great admiration how Colin took weekly RE classes (Religious Education) in Silkstone State Primary School. He took all classes, all levels, on his own. There were no lay teachers in those times. In the upper school, the classrooms were divided by concertina doors that could be pushed back allowing several rooms to become one huge one. Week after week, Colin faithfully taught us "rabble" packed in tightly from wall to wall and back to front. Anglicans were by far the nominal majority and Silkstone School was the largest state school in Queensland. Colin's sincerity and passion as he taught us in Confirmation class was "catching". I remember his exhorting us to pray for our future partner, to find the right husband or wife - the one that God had already chosen for "me". That became my prayer until the day I found "that one" in Tom, my husband of fifty-seven years this year of 2021.

I continued to worship God every chance I had, going to church at 6.20 am each Sunday morning (that odd time so the churches "down the line" could also have services each week), followed by Sunday School teaching and then each Sunday night at Evensong. I even went at 6.30 am on Saints days through the week. I can't recall the year, but Colin arranged a Church Army Mission in the church. Under Captain Roy Buckingham's ministry, I made a public confession of my faith.

Then came the Billy Graham Crusade in 1959. I trained as a Counsellor with Miriam Chantrill who later went as a missionary to the Northern Territory with CMS. The Scriptures I learnt anchored me in my walk of faith. At around this time, I met my husband to be. We were introduced outside All Saints' Church one Sunday night and I instantly "knew" he was the one God had planned for me. I told no one but waited and prayed for God to work it all out in His time.

In my senior high school years, I became involved in CMS League of Youth. Under Rev Jeff and Ursula Roper my faith was further nurtured as they loved and taught many of us youth during their years of faithful ministry in southern Queensland. Child Evangelism Fellowship and Scripture Union were also very significant in my journey. At Scarborough Beach Mission, which I attended for many years, our houseparents were Ma and Pa Kilvert. Ma prayer counselled me regarding my childhood traumas and 1 John 1:9 was very cathartic for me.

On Saturday mornings, we young people would spontaneously gravitate to the church. We would pray together and share the Scripture nuggets God had given us that week and their relevance to our faith journey with Jesus. We encouraged one another. After Sunday Evensong, many of us would continue fellowshipping and sharing at a sing-along in a home with a piano, usually at the Chantrills' home. I learnt many hymns and songs that I still love to sing.

Colin and Judith's ministry and teaching were strengthening and developing my faith as they exemplified Christ's teaching and discipled our growing church. Then in 1961, the blow came. Colin announced they were leaving the Parish for St Stephen's Newtown in Sydney. I felt devastated and so did many others. I remember Tom and I met for prayer in the church. We were crying out to God for help and as we searched the Scriptures, He showed us Phil. 2:12 (RSV), encouraging us to henceforth "work out your own salvation with fear and trembling". We took those words to heart and prayed earnestly for the man or couple that God would give us in Colin and Judith's place.

When Rev Don and Margaret Douglass arrived at All Saints' Booval a new era of ministry began. They faithfully built on the foundation laid by Colin and Judith. Don's preaching and teaching was solid and grounding, his stutter was barely noticeable as he faithfully proclaimed God's word each week. Margaret kept the home fires burning while supporting Don's ministry. She established a thriving Young Wives group many of whom found faith and grew spiritually under their ministry. It was a privilege to babysit for them and to share their family life sometimes, even going on holiday with them to Hastings Point one year. What a fun time I had, especially boating with them on the river!

In 1960 I was one of the last of the one-year trained teachers at Kelvin Grove Teachers College. I was on a government scholarship and bonded to teach for 3 years after my training. Bob and Olive Robertson had responded to God's call to missionary service in the

Northern Territory and so had Brian and Miriam Chantrill under Colin's ministry. I too was seriously seeking what God's assignment was for my life. I investigated whether I could convert my three-year bond into missionary teaching in the Northern Territory but to no avail. When Brian Chantrill went to Sydney Missionary and Bible College before going north, my curiosity was aroused. As I contemplated my future, I wondered. By this time, my relationship with Tom was also fluttering in the wings but we both determined to do what God wanted and in His time.

After completing three years teaching and after much prayer, I decided to head to Sydney Missionary and Bible College where, once again, I was able (with Tom) to work each Sunday with Colin and Judith in the Parish of St Stephen's Newtown – a very run-down inner city mission parish with a high migrant population. What a thrilling and unique experience we had in being able to start an open air Sunday School in Georgina Street park with the local migrant children – a work that continued for many, many years after we moved on. I owe much to the scriptural grounding and experience of life, ministry and mission I received that year at SMBC in an atmosphere of love, discipline and quality teaching.

Heather Rasmussen at Georgina Street Park Open Air Sunday School Newtown Sydney 1964

The Pearl of Great Price has been worth every step of my journey with Him.

Of later years I have also come to see the merchantman as God the Father who loves me so much that He gave all for me. He counted *me as a "pearl of great price"* so much so that He gave His only Son, even to death on a cross, so that by His redemption I am His beloved daughter both now and in eternity.

I am eternally grateful to Jesus, **The Pearl of Great Price** as well as for being **His pearl of great price**. I praise God also for All Saints' Booval for nurturing and nourishing my early faith.

TOM AND HEATHER JOURNEY TOGETHER

> *"O magnify the LORD with me and let us exalt His Name together." (This was the theme for our wedding and our future.)*
>
> — PSALM 34:3 (RSV)

At the end of 1964 we returned home to Booval to be married at All Saints' by Don Douglass and Jim Stonier on the 12th hour of the 12th day of the 12th month in the little wooden church filled with so many memories for both of us. Jim Holbeck and Carole Tapsell were our best man and bridesmaid.

Until we left for Ridley, we were temporary caretakers for the newly acquired Griffith House - a purchase spearheaded by Margaret Douglass through the Queensland Mental Welfare Association and used to support the transition of folk from Wolston Park back into the community – another outreach ministry of parishioners from All Saints'.

We had forty pounds between us and all our belongings fitted into an old FJ Holden when we set out from Brisbane for Tom to study at Ridley College Melbourne. For two years we lived in a bed-sitter in East Ivanhoe and then for two years in married accommodation at the College, first in a single room in a shared house. Then in an old army hut we had three very small rooms which we loved and which always seemed full of other students visiting - "coffeeing", fellowshipping and having discussions.

On Sundays, Tom gained practical training and experience as a Catechist in various parishes as well as valuable experience at the Mission to Seamen in South Melbourne. Heather taught at both Hawthorn West Central and Flemington High Schools while Tom studied over this 4-year period.

During his final year, Tom accepted an offer for ordination in the Diocese of Melbourne. In 1969 he was ordained deacon in St Paul's Cathedral and appointed as curate to St George's Mont Albert in the Parish of Holy Trinity Surrey Hills. Here we learnt some valuable lessons about prayer. In 1970 the first of our three beautiful daughters was born through prayer. A parishioner introduced us to the Order of St Luke which focuses on the healing prayer ministry. At CFO (Camp Farthest Out) we experienced God at work in the whole of our daily lives - our work can truly be our worship. We experienced several weeks of CFO where every day was blended in prayer through the meals, exercise, creative activities, personal and group prayer, talks and personal interactions. This has been so meaningful to us in our walk of faith.

| Tom Wood and Heather Rasmussen 1962

Ros Rinker's book, *Prayer, Conversing with God*, opened our eyes to faith-sized requests. God's constant practical provision for us has been very humbling. Over the years, in answer to prayer, we have twice anonymously received large amounts of money just as needed. Twice we have received potatoes! Once, Heather, telling no one, prayed for potatoes. The pantry was empty and she needed some for Sunday lunch. Her parents were visiting and her Dad always expected potatoes for a roast meal. He loved to sit on the brick wall surrounding the Rectory watching the traffic going by. Would you believe it, that day he came back inside with an armful of potatoes and said, "These just fell off a truck passing by. Could you use them?" Yes, God has a sense of humour and the little things matter to God too.

After a second curacy at Blackburn where our second daughter was born, Tom became the Vicar of St Mark's Reservoir. Reminiscent of our own teenage years at Booval, we saw the Holy Spirit move among the young people under the leadership of Graeme Littleton who walked the streets of Reservoir relating to the youth. After the film *King of Kings* (black and white version) was shown at a camp, the Holy Spirit fell on these young people with much weeping, repentance and turning to Christ. They came back to the church on fire for God and they would meet in the church for prayer. They invited their friends and led them to Christ. They led worship services on a Sunday night. Several dedicated their lives for other ministries such as YWAM (Youth with a Mission). One couple became cross-cultural missionaries.

In 1973, at the invitation of Archbishop Felix Arnott, Tom accepted a curacy at St Alban's Goodna (with Riverview and Redbank). On two occasions friends with spiritual discernment gave us a warning that dark days lay ahead. Shortly afterwards Goodna and other parts of Brisbane were inundated with flooding. First Woogaroo Creek became a swirling wall of water that swept through the caravan park and other low-lying areas. The police knocked us up around midnight to open up the church and hall to take in the people being rescued by all available local boats. We organised blankets, pillows and food and we kept the kettle boiling for the cups and cups of tea and coffee needed to warm the victims. By Saturday lunch the creek had abated, but late Saturday the Brisbane River broke its banks and once again we were in emergency mode with rising water. This time we were cut off for days from the rest of the world.

The highway was cut and the shopping centre gradually went under. Tom and a few others emptied each shop as the waters continued to rise. One of the bank's employees organized the men to remove important files and documents and store them in our garage. The supermarket stock was stored in our little church. By Sunday it was impossible to see the cross on the altar but this food proved a boon as we meted it out to needy families. With no electricity, Heather, at 8 months pregnant, took on the task of cooking in the open air with only the boilers and dixies provided by the Army. People stored as much clean water as possible – in baths, sinks, tubs, buckets. Eventually even our water supply was lost as concerns arose that it was contaminated.

When the waters receded, the clean- up began. Out of nowhere came "Dad's Army" - a force of volunteers from all over who dedicated their time, labour and sweat to the massive task of removing mud, furniture and belongings and to washing and scrubbing homes and buildings.

Within a few weeks, our third daughter was born. Days were full and hectic but God used the flood to begin to build the church. The first Sunday service afterwards, the little church at St Alban's was packed. Some found faith, or a deeper faith in Christ, but many needed sustained care and support. Tom, as one of the community appointees for post flood recovery was thrust into an extremely busy time of visitation and organising of practical help to so many families. He spent hours in counselling folk who had been deeply affected by their losses and the strain that was placed on relationships.

At the end of that year Tom was invited to become Rector of St Andrew's South Brisbane where we served a very diverse and eclectic congregation for the next ten years. Many parishioners lived outside the boundaries of the parish, their spiritual roots having been laid in previous generations by parents or grandparents worshipping there. Family baptisms and marriages were traditional. On the other hand, the surrounding inner-city area had gradually been changing and those who lived locally were often poor, lived in rented accommodation and relied heavily on government support. To marry the two cultures we needed to embrace both and to make the locals feel welcome.

We found that sharing meals was a very important part of local outreach. On Sunday evenings, a small band of parishioners would bring soup, finger food and easy dishes to the "Blue Room" under the church's main building. This meal was followed by an informal relaxed worship time that became very special for everyone involved. Many friendships were formed and a supportive community evolved. The Rectory too became an open house for Sunday breakfasts and on Christmas Day every year local folk came to share our own Christmas meal. At times we had fifty people celebrating with our family.

In 1985 Tom left parish ministry and started his own counselling practice, a risky undertaking. With Expo 88, we became house parents to all the local and international guides for the Pavilion of Promise. We eventually moved back to Ipswich for the next ten years. Tom looked after a little Congregational Church for a while before starting to work for the Bible Society, a work he loved. All over Queensland and Northern New South Wales, he ministered in every denomination and visited many supporters before becoming a Funeral Celebrant. This was a fruitful time of ministry to the wider community followed by some locum work. Eventually he worked as a public servant for the Queensland Government before retirement.

Throughout our journey and still today we go back to what Colin and Judith Ware, Don and Margaret Douglass and Jim Stonier taught and modelled both in ministry and marriage and we thank God our Father for all of them. Truly the Kingdom of God broke into our lives during those years at All Saints' Booval. We are so looking forward to that great day when we will all be together in heaven rejoicing with God our Father.

14

JOHN MCNAMEE
RECOLLECTIONS OF ALL SAINTS' BOOVAL

Rev John and Mrs Glynis McNamee's 50th Wedding Anniversary 2013

I GREW UP AT CAITHNESS STREET NORTH BOOVAL, THE SON of Daniel and Mary McNamee and older brother of Joyce.

I have many vivid childhood memories of services that have

disappeared with the passing of time. Once the ice man would deliver the ice for the ice chest, the milkman would deliver milk in round one pint bottles, the baker would deliver fresh bread and even the fruit and vegetables merchants would regularly make their rounds. However a bus trip into Ipswich was still required to buy other items that Mum would bring home in her string bags.

As time went by, I learnt to ride a bicycle and I was able to go to the butcher to buy fresh meat for the family. That was just on the other side of the Ipswich to Brisbane railway line which divided North Booval from the remainder of Booval. All Saints' Booval was a bit further south on Station Road where it was crossed by Brisbane Road. In those days, that was outside the area in which I was allowed to ride my bike.

Fast-forward a couple of years - Dad now had a better car and we started going to church on Sundays at the nice wooden church called All Saints'. I started attending Sunday School in the hall just behind the church. Then the family started attending the Holy Communion service fairly regularly. I was prepared for Confirmation by Kenneth Watts, using the Catechism from the Book of Common Prayer. It began in a rather curious way, "*Question. What is your name? Answer N. or M.*" (*1662 Book of Common Prayer*) But my name was John. It was a rather strange question for an eleven-year-old boy to get his head around. But our priest persevered so that we could almost recite the catechism by heart before we were confirmed by Archbishop Halse on Sunday, 1st August 1954.

After confirmation our family continued to attend church regularly. I learnt many of the hymns and after we arrived home I would often go under our high-set house and sit on the swing and sing some of the hymns we had sung in church and some of my other favourites. In church I noticed the number of elderly people who were following the service in the same pocket sized Prayer Book I was using. The print was so fine, I wondered how they could read it. Looking back, I guess they knew the service by heart.

A little later, I became a scout in the Fifth Ipswich Scout Group at Booval, and I also started attending youth groups at All

Saints' Booval. I was introduced to the "Four Square" program planned by the group itself to include the Spiritual, Physical, Mental and Social aspects. YAF (Young Anglican Fellowship) did this very well. There was also a CMS League of Youth group at All Saints'. These two groups started me on the path to considering ministry as much as a teenage boy could. Through YAF and CMS and their camps, that challenge grew. I was deeply impressed by the way Colin Ware and Don Douglass conducted worship and by their passionate devotion to the gospel. However, being alongside people like Greg Ezzy and Tom Wood as well as a couple of the girls who seemed to know their Bibles very well, I never thought of ministry in a really serious way. I felt lacking.

At this time I started going out with Glynis Renton, who keenly attended St Thomas' North Ipswich each Sunday. Her father had been a Lay Reader in the church at Killarney, near Warwick where he had served as a policeman. He died when Glynis was about five and she and her mother had moved to Ipswich where her brother Elwyn was born shortly afterwards.

Glynis continued worshipping at St. Thomas' North Ipswich and I continued to worship at All Saints'. We did not like that arrangement very much, so for a while we attended St. Paul's Ipswich. Over time, and with encouragement from Glynis, I became more interested in a ministry role in the church. The daughter church in St. Paul's parish needed an organist for the Sunday School as well as a Superintendent. Glynis could play the piano, so she began to play hymns for the Sunday School and I taught a class. I also became a CEBS leader and later became Superintendent of the Sunday School.

In time I joined the Postulants' Guild, a group formed to help young men decide whether they were being called to ordained ministry or some other role. This was led by the Rev Keith Rayner, who later became Primate of the Australian Anglican Church. At that time there was the possibility of serving in Bush Ministry for three or so years as a single man after becoming a priest or, if the person was married, of waiting the same amount of time before ordination. Glynis and I chose marriage. I felt I needed more time to finish my apprenticeship and gain some trade skills. In those days there was pressure to "have a trade to fall back on if necessary".

After a number of years working in the motor mechanic trade, I had progressed through the ranks to be a foreman, service advisor and workshop manager. I then became a manual arts teacher at "Churchie" (now Anglican Grammar School) in Brisbane. After approximately five years there, I transitioned to become a TAFE trade teacher in Townsville where I met Doug Wellington, the parish priest at West End, Townsville.

After many long chats with Doug, I became Eucharistic Assistant and he introduced me to the North Queensland Bishop, John Lewis. Bishop Lewis had been the principal of a Theological College before being consecrated Bishop of North Queensland. He personally directed me to courses to prepare me for ordination. However, before that could happen, TAFE transferred me to Ipswich and I returned to All Saints' Booval. Kevin Ellem was locum at the time and later became Rector. I also met John Nicholls there. Later we both served together as assistant priests at St. James' Toowoomba.

Bishop Lewis asked me to return to North Queensland and to continue preparation for ordination. Early in 1979 I was made a Deacon and stationed at St. Peter's West End, Townsville under the direction of the Cathedral Ministry Centre. Every Wednesday morning Bishop Lewis conducted a healing service at St. Peter's. The week after I was made a deacon, I attended that service since I was living next door. The following week the Bishop phoned me an hour before the Wednesday service and told me something had come up and he would not be able to be there. He asked if I would lead the service and gave me a ten-minute instruction on what I was to do. To cut a long story short, it was successful and I conducted that service for the remainder of my time at St. Peter's. On the 4th November 1979 I was ordained Priest in St. James' Cathedral, Townsville.

In the meantime I had been studying Education with an emphasis on Religious Education. Bishop Lewis thought it would be a good idea if I went to All Souls' Anglican School at Charters' Towers. I had been informed that this was a good Christian school. How wrong I was! It turned out that the Headmaster loved the toughness of the English Grammar School system and believed all the staff should too. All staff were issued with a leather strap and told to use it if any student misbehaved. This went against my principles. Instead, I would make students who misbehaved talk through the incident. (One tough senior boy who boasted as a matter of pride that he had managed to get every other teacher to use the strap on him, complained that I was spoiling his record of toughness.) I was given a couple of classes to teach Religious Education but most of my work involved administration.

Preaching at one of the school chapel services, I quoted the Matthew Henry Commentary recommended by the Bishop for St Peter's parish to buy me as an ordination present. The Principal and the local priest disapproved of this and complained to the Bishop.

I was then sent to St James' Toowoomba where Canon Thomas was the Rector.

Canon Thomas asked me to coordinate Religious Education in twenty-one schools in the parish, supervising the lay teachers and providing teaching materials. I also taught Religious Education in the Glennie Anglican Girls School in Toowoomba where the head teacher asked me to broaden the curriculum to include all religions. This was a quite a challenge, but I was able to do this.

The years since Toowoomba include ministry for two years at Tara Parish and for eight years at Jandowae Parish (the longest incumbency ever at Jandowae) and a further few years teaching in schools. In retirement I am still active in ministry in the Mudgeeraba Parish where I am currently licensed as PTO retired. From time to time I also help out in the Gold Coast North Parish.

My wife Glynis died in August 2019 after a long battle with Parkinson's disease. We found great comfort in God's unfailing love. In Romans 8:38 and 39, Paul wrote, *"For I am certain that nothing can separate us from his (God's) love: neither death nor life, neither angels nor other heavenly rulers or powers, neither the present nor the future, neither the world above nor the world below - there is nothing in all creation that will ever be able to separate us from the love of God which is ours through Christ Jesus our Lord."* (TEV)

If we put that belief at the centre of our lives it *is* possible to defeat every adversity that the world or the evil one may throw at us, even death. We can overcome any obstacle in Jesus our Saviour.

In conclusion, I, and my children and their spouses, wish All Saints' Booval every success and God's blessing on all members past, present and future. In Jesus' name we thank All Saints' Booval for the inspiration they gave to start me on the road to ordination and a life in God's service.

15

JUNE SINGLETON

RECOLLECTIONS OF ALL SAINT'S BOOVAL
(WITH GEOFFREY)

| Geoffrey and June Singleton

MY HUSBAND, GEOFFREY SINGLETON AND I, JUNE Singleton, now live in Aveo Retirement Village in Durack, but we want to share some memories of All Saints' Booval between 1959 and 1969 and our subsequent life here.

Our close friend, Jim Stonier, who taught with Geoff at Ipswich Grammar School, invited us to attend the Billy Graham Crusade in Brisbane in 1959. I had only been to church for my sister's wedding and for our own in 1958 and had never read the Bible. Geoff had attended St Andrew's Lutwyche and had been confirmed. We both went forward that night and our lives changed! We were directed to All Saints' Booval and wow! What a wonderful hive of Christians!

Soon after, when gardening in our home in Schelbach Street, we saw a minister get off his push bike at our gate... Colin Ware! No fancy car or cold distant phone call, but he, himself. He was such a humble, loving man and he welcomed us to All Saints'. His wife, Judith, was just the sweetest, kindest person and we felt welcomed by all. We were helped to read the Bible and to learn passages which I can still remember today! I was confirmed in 1959 at St Pauls in Ipswich - the Rector there was the Rev Kestell Cornish.

At All Saints', the church services were always full of the Spirit. We went to Holy Communion when we could - especially a problem when breast feeding babies! We really loved the Evensong, but as the children would be in bed, one of us stayed home. We loved Rev Ware's sermons and then came Rev Don Douglass and Margaret. What fantastic Christians, so certain and positive! Margaret was leader of our MU and Young Wives and was very enthusiastic.

My time with our Lord started at All Saints', reading Scripture Union's Daily Bread which I still read today. Our Bible is stained and frayed but has weathered well. Jim Stonier gave it to us in 1962 with the words from Psalm 119:105, "Thy word is a lamp to my feet and a light to my path." and that's what it really has been. Sometimes, over the years, that light has become a little faint but, once back on the path, the light is still there.

Then dear Mrs Marjorie Porter asked us to help in the kindergarten Sunday School. This was in the little hall at the back and Mrs Wallis ran it. Though a very young Christian, I learnt so much from telling the children about our Lord. Geoff made a sand pit on a stand and we often enacted Bible scenes in the sand. The main Sunday School was in the big hall where Mrs Porter was in charge of hundreds of young people, or so it seemed. Initially using the Cradle Roll, Mrs Wallis later started the daily Pre-

School/Kindergarten catering for the littlies. This outreach ministry operated for many, many years and was especially helpful to the large number of young mums.

Happy days! I had our 3 children, Craig, Melanie and Donald in 3 years from 1961. Everyone was so supportive. Mrs Porter often looked after Craig following Melanie and Donald's births – no fuss, just plenty of advice. Mrs Ada Fay came every afternoon about 5pm and bathed my three toddlers then went straight home afterwards – no idle chatter. Individuals like these demonstrated a personal caring ministry. We remember the church picnics, fairs and the cake stalls.

June Singleton with Craig (on seat), Donald (on lap) and Melanie (on small seat) and Kerry Frith (in front) early 1960s

At All Saints' there was a dynamic group of young people and we asked Heather Rasmussen (now Mrs Tom Wood) to be Godmother to our daughter Melanie and Jim Holbeck to be Godfather to our younger son Donald. Our old friend Jim Stonier, who later became the curate, was Godfather to our eldest child, Craig. The two Jims became Clergymen and Heather's husband, Tom, also entered the ministry!

We still keep in touch. In 2019 we drove to Port Macquarie and visited Jim and Carole Holbeck and attended Jim's Healing Service at the old St Thomas' Church where my grandparents had been married and my mother had been baptised. They were wonderful to us. Carole was truly walking with the Lord and, like her dear mother Mrs Tapsell, who also played the organ and worshipped at All Saints', her Christian example will never be forgotten. Sadly for Jim and those in this world, Carole went to our Lord soon afterwards and rose to glory.

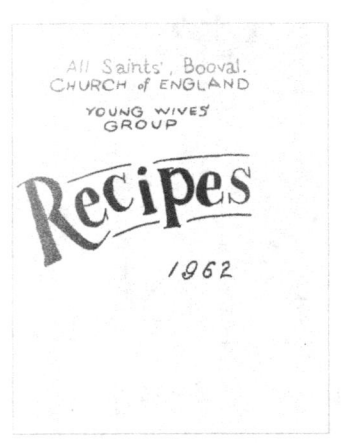

All Saints' Booval Young Wives' Recipe Book 1962

We attended CMS camps at Mount Tamborine with the Rev Jeff Roper and I remember joining Mothers Union in 1959 or 1960. Our MU used to go as a group to visit Goodna Mental Hospital. We had a Cradle Roll organised by Mrs Wallis and we called on all mothers of newly baptised babies, inviting them to church and showing them we cared. We started a Young Wives Group, knocking on doors and inviting folk to join. We, the Young Wives, even had a tennis club once a week. In those days wives mostly stayed home and looked after the children, so we had lots of babies and toddlers. Margaret Douglass encouraged us to compile our own Recipe Book which we printed and sold, with the proceeds going to All Saints'. I still have mine and remember with great fondness the members who contributed.

As a result of our "drive" for new young wives, Geoff and I met

Ken and Tricia Frith who lived not far from us. So a friendship started which has lasted until today. We have visited each other over the years even in different states. Tricia is very active at her church south of Adelaide and is MU President and Liturgical Assistant there. Seeds were sown at All Saints'...some we may never see grow but I am sure there are many healthy plants still growing...now adults, serving the Lord.

Geoff taught for eleven years at Ipswich Grammar School and for over twenty at Brisbane Grammar School. After further study, I followed him into education, teaching at Indooroopilly State High School for seventeen years. After living in retirement at Maleny for thirteen years, we moved back to Brisbane.

Shortly after we came here, I started a Christian Library with 4 books! Over 10 years it grew to over 1000 books, mostly donated by residents. I also wrote a weekly Christian Book Review for those 10 years and it was printed in our weekly paper, *The Breeze*. I still do a Book Review but only once a month.

Once or twice a year I have organised a "Gathering" of all Christians of all denominations in the Village. Each denomination is represented in reading scripture, with 2 hymns after each reading. About 50 attend and the rafters are lifted off! Unfortunately, we had no "Gathering" in 2020 because of COVID but hopefully we will again in 2021!

I also teach art here - watercolour, oil and acrylic, once a week. We display our works (about thirty each time) every 3 months in the Village. It brings great joy to the artists, many just beginners of average age 80 plus. To spread the Gospel, I always paint 4 or 5 Christian paintings at Easter and Christmas and many residents have told me how much they appreciate this as most decorations here at Easter and Christmas lack any Christian content. I have also painted small nativity scenes to give away at Christmas and many now have them displayed in their windows. More seeds? I praise God for this "hidden" talent discovered when I retired.

I believe that prayer is essential for everything - for health, healing, guidance, strength and for fellowship with God and our Lord. We can do nothing without God's help and guidance. "Take it to The Lord in prayer". So often I have thought I could do it alone…result…disaster!

My hope and prayer for God's church is that we will focus on the Word and the power of The Trinity - of God our Father, of our Lord Jesus and of the Holy Spirit. My prayer is that parish councils and parishioners will concentrate on spreading the Gospel, promoting Bible studies and prayer meetings, on reaching out to the community as Jesus did – to the sick, to the outcasts such as drug and alcohol addicts, to the homeless, to the lonely and to the abused. We need to listen to all and be compassionate but firm in our Christian beliefs. There is an urgent need to pray for our Church leaders, our Premiers and our Prime Minister, that they may receive wisdom and guidance from God. In particular we need to pray that people will understand that they are not saved by being nice and good, but by believing in Jesus who is more powerful than the devil and who is the only way to eternal life.

Geoff and I are so grateful for the examples and love of all who attended All Saints' so many years ago. May we all persevere in following Jesus.

> "Those who wait on the Lord shall renew their strength,
>> they shall mount up with wings like eagles,
>> they shall run and not be weary,
>> they shall walk and not faint."
>
> — ISAIAH 40:31 (NKJV)

16

BILL AND HILARY SAUNDERS
MEMORIES OF ALL SAINTS' BOOVAL

Bill Saunders (centre) and others paddling canoes built by All Saints' Booval CEBS early 1960s

BILL:

My first memory of All Saints' was attending CEBS (Church of England Boys Society) when I was about 10. We lived in Stafford Street and my family attended Bundamba Church, but I joined CEBS at All Saints' and can remember running there and back home in the dark by myself. I really enjoyed CEBS and stayed with the organisation into my 20's.

Our family started attending All Saints' when we moved to Brisbane Road and family life revolved around the church. I have great memories of church soccer, church cricket (with Rev Colin Ware as Umpire) and Sunday School picnics when the whole church took the train to Shorncliffe. I was confirmed and became an altar boy travelling with the minister of the day to the various parish churches. I often carried the cross on special occasions because I couldn't be tempted to smile! We attended services both morning and night and our dog, Boy, often snuck down and sat under our pew until the service ended.

I have most vivid memories of Rev Colin Ware and Rev Don Douglass who found time to actually visit families in their homes. My favourite memory is of a project we undertook at the church in our late teens to construct canoes, under the leadership of Mr Burt. We then paddled these, under the leadership of Rev Brian Seers, from the Bremer River to Brisbane, drawing the attention of the local news. I am grateful for the leadership of these godly men who successfully navigated us through our teenage years.

HILARY:

I first attended All Saints' Church while going out with Bill. We met at a CMS Summer School at Port Macquarie in 1965. Later on, I occasionally stayed over at the Saunders' residence under strict supervision. Attending church was mandatory. The "old" church of All Saints' was very similar to my home church at Wavell Heights, but the noticeable difference was the numbers of people attending and in particular, the numbers of people our age – early twenties.

The Church was very much alive with lots of opportunities to be involved. One of our first duties after we were married was to be house parents at a church camp. Our children were all baptized there and when they attended Sunday School, I joined the ranks as a teacher of the younger ones. I remember many families – the Stephens, the Roses, the Wallis family, the McGraths, the Barrells, the Bertlings, the Lists and more.

I look back with happy memories of the church we attended until the 1980s – of morning teas, suppers, picnics, dinners and fetes. Mostly I remember All Saints' as a vibrant community of people who truly loved and served the Lord.

BOTH OF US:

A lot of water has gone under the bridge since then. We have been conscious of God's goodness and faithfulness through our many happy years and some seriously challenging times. We have continued to serve Him in varying capacities, myself in Christian schooling and Sunday School with both of us in Alice Springs. We now live in the Sunshine Coast hinterland and are active members of Suncoast Church. His Word continues to be *the lamp to our feet and the light to our path*.

Happy Anniversary All Saints'! God bless!

17

PATRICIA FRITH
RECOLLECTIONS OF ALL SAINTS' BOOVAL

All Saints' Booval Tennis Club 1960s. 2nd row R Tricia Frith and Front Row R June Singleton

KEN AND I WERE NEWLY MARRIED WHEN WE MOVED TO Booval for two years in November 1963. I had just completed nursing training at the Adelaide Children's Hospital. Ken had been commissioned as a RAAF officer and posted to Amberley Base. Our rental property had a large lawn, a banana palm and a backyard toilet. We were starting from scratch and needed a lawn mower before a car! Ken bought me a dog for company as he spent long days at the base and depended on public transport. I found adjusting to the wet and dry seasons of Queensland quite challenging on top of being pregnant.

Soon after our daughter Kerry was born, we began to attend All Saints' Booval. What a hive of activity! A visit from Mothers Union followed and MU introduced me to June Singleton. We have become lifelong friends.

Don and Margaret Douglass whetted my appetite for missions and helped to develop my church and family life.

After two years at Amberley, Ken was posted to Laverton in Victoria. In 1970-1 we spent 15months in Mawson Antarctica where Ken was installing radiotelephones. Ken retired from the Air Force in 1978 and we moved to an almond orchard at Willunga, south of Adelaide. Ken died in 2001.

I continue to serve the Lord in the local church and as a MU leader in the Southern Vales within the Murray Diocese. Outreach and fund raising through rose pruning is my thing!

My prayer and hope for the church is for more home group fellowships and Bible study as well as greater support for missions and community service. That's what was so exciting and effective at Booval!

18

DOUG WISKAR

MEMORIES OF ALL SAINTS' BOOVAL

My memories of All Saints' Booval during this period are of a parish with a congregation active in worship and involved in the general operation of the parish.

I have fond memories of so many people, Mrs Porter, the Bridley family, the Rasmussens, Alwyn and Dell Smith, the Barrells, Millicent and Alwyn Rose to name just a few. For many, many years, Mr Rose made the regularly changing eye-catching signage at the church entrance.

During the early part of 1958, with the guidance and enthusiastic support of the Rev Colin Ware and under the leadership of Graham and Enid Markcrow, a branch of the Young Anglican Fellowship was established at All Saints' Booval. The group met on a Friday night, that being a suitable time slot for members who were students. There were discussions on scripture and doctrine together with varying social activities. Each YAF meeting closed with the service of Compline in the church and was usually led by Rev Colin Ware and/or the group leaders.

Visits by Booval YAF to other parishes occurred. Some All Saints' members also enjoyed camps run by the Diocesan Young Anglican Fellowship, the first of which took place late in 1958.

Friendships established within YAF and at YAF camps have continued to the present day.

My present parish is St Hugh's Inala. My wife, Gloria, and myself are both Lay Assistants. Currently, my family and I worship with the St Hugh's/Aveo Durack chapel community even though we don't live in the Aveo village.

19

ALAN AND BETH WOOLARD
OUR JOURNEY – "RIPPLES IN TIME AND SPACE"

| Dr Alan and Mrs Beth Woolard

WE WERE BOTH BORN IN 1953 AND SPENT THE FIRST 24 years of our lives in Ipswich. We married in December 1977 at the same time as Alan graduated from Medicine at the University of Queensland and we commenced our married life in Brisbane. We have three adult daughters, one granddaughter and, at the time of writing, another grandchild on the way.

We look back on our time at All Saints' Booval with very fond memories. This was where we became Christians and where the foundations for our walk with Christ were established.

Fortunately, the Holy Spirit had not departed All Saints' after 1965. His work continued and the fruit of the previous decade was evident.

ALAN

One of my earliest memories of my connection with All Saints' was of my younger brother looking at me in bed as I feigned sleep. It was a Sunday morning and I was hoping that my mother wouldn't have the heart to wake me and send me to Sunday School. My brother was on the ball and declared, "He's not asleep! I can see him breathing!" While demonstrating a certain naivety in regard to the physiology of sleep, he was correct in his diagnosis. Fortunately for my long term good, my mother was a strong-willed godly woman. So, I went to Sunday School and to CEBS (Church of England Boys Society). Though I never doubted that there was a God, I didn't come to know Christ as my Lord and Saviour until my confirmation year. I was about 12 years old and it was about 1966. God gave me a yearning for spiritual knowledge at that time but I was on the verge of being led astray by a zealous Jehovah's Witness. Fortunately, my Sunday School teacher at that point was Alwyn Rose, one of the finest servants of God that I have ever known. He was God's human instrument in my coming to a personal faith in Christ, reassuring me of my salvation and helping establish the building blocks for spiritual growth.

At 15 years of age, I joined the All Saints' Youth Club. I owe an enormous debt of gratitude to the leaders and senior members of that group. I'll always treasure their friendship, kindness and forbearance as they modelled Christ and helped me grow in the faith.

I can say the same for the wider fellowship of the body of Christ at Booval under the leadership, at that time, of the Rev Herb Robey. Rev Don Campbell was one of the curates for a time and he was also an enormous blessing. I also treasure the witness and fellowship of so many families – the Roses, Poultons, Smiths,

McGraths, Macleans, Extons, the Wallis family, the Campbells, Tapsells and Bridleys. Through this body of Christ, the Gospel was preached and lived. The Bible was taught. Evangelism, discipleship, service, pastoral care and cross-cultural mission were practised and encouraged.

Another form of ministry with a connection to All Saints' was Christian folk music, embodied by the group "The Coaltown Revival". Three of the four members of the group were members of the All Saints' Youth Club and proclaimed Christ at various venues and Christian coffee clubs.

The parish was a hive of activity with youth teas, men's and ladies' dinners, Mothers Union, Bible studies for various ages, social events, youth camps, parish camps and youth services. Through it all, I became familiar with Scripture Union Bible reading aids and learnt the discipline of daily Bible reading and prayer while exploring various types of service. I became involved in a Christian group at school (ISCF), Scripture Union beach missions and League of Youth (a mission minded youth and young adults' group associated with the Church Missionary Society).

BETH

My parents attended All Saints' Booval from when I was young. My siblings and I went to Sunday School and I was a part of GFS (Girls Friendly Society) and my older brother attended CEBS as Alan did. I remember enjoying my involvement in these activities. I have particularly fond memories of Mrs Tapsell, a Sunday School teacher, who also encouraged and taught me to play the organ in my mid to late teens.

Lesley McGrath (now Woodley) was one of my GFS leaders in my early teens and was important in my spiritual growth. I can remember acknowledging Jesus as my Saviour during a GFS camp at Mt Tamborine. During my teens, I attended church and GFS, became a Sunday School teacher and played the organ for some services. These were more in the nature of commitments rather than service for Christ, as I don't remember giving Him a place in my decisions at that time.

However, when Lesley was home on leave she spoke at the Youth Group. I had responded to an invitation to attend. During the study on 1 Peter 1, God confronted me. He challenged me to look at my life and His place in it. From that time, Jesus was not just my Saviour but was my Lord as well. I started going to the Youth Group and I was challenged to know the Bible more. This led me to attend Monday evening lectures at a theological college (BCQ Toowong). Later, I also did some correspondence study via Moore College while Alan completed his medical course. Alan also introduced me to League of Youth and CMS where serving God took on a new direction as our relationship grew. Like Alan, I also valued the fellowship and encouragement from the family of God at All Saints' and felt that they gave me opportunities to grow in faith and service while there.

ALAN AND BETH

After getting married in December 1977, we moved to Brisbane and joined another evangelical Anglican Church – St Stephen's Coorparoo. The probability of overseas missionary service was in our minds as Alan commenced work as a doctor. He worked at the Brisbane Mater Hospital for three years from 1978. Our first daughter, Kim, was born in 1980. We moved to Bundaberg in 1981 and Alan worked at the hospital for one year to obtain some basic surgical experience.

In 1982, we moved to Melbourne and studied at Ridley Theological College for one year. We then attended St. Andrew's Hall (the CMS training college) for the first half of 1983. Our second daughter, Debra, was born in June 1983.

Subsequently, we left Australia with our three-month-old and three-year-old daughters to work as CMS missionaries in Tanzania, East Africa. This was a particularly difficult and heartbreaking period, especially for our parents. They knew they would miss out on the next three years of their young granddaughters' lives as we would not return to Australia until the end of 1986. This was in the era without emails and social media and with very poor international phone service in East Africa.

We studied Swahili at a language school in Kenya for three months and then Alan commenced work as a medical missionary at Mvumi (of Paul White, Jungle Doctor fame) in the centre of Tanzania. This was a very stressful time as Alan felt extremely ill equipped to manage the breadth and depth of medical problems encountered. Fortunately, we worked in a fellowship of Tanzanian and international Christians and had the prayerful support of the CMS family and churches in Australia, especially All Saints' Booval and St. Stephen's Coorparoo. We were encouraged by the verse *My grace is sufficient for you, for my power is made perfect in weakness.* (2 Corinthians 12:9 NIV)

On completion of our service with CMS, Alan commenced work in a group general practice in Brisbane in May 1987 and has continued there to this day. Our third daughter, Lisa, was also born in 1987.

We returned to our Brisbane home church at St. Stephen's Coorparoo. Alan became honorary medical advisor to CMS Qld/Northern NSW for several years. We also helped lead a CMS youth and young adults mission interest group (called Cross Culture) for a number of years. It was a joy working with young people who have gone on to serve Christ in full time or voluntary ministry both here and overseas. *You will be my witnesses in Jerusalem, and in all Judea and Samaria, and to the ends of the earth.* (Acts 1:8 NIV)

At St Stephen's, we became involved in various ministries – parish council, music ministry, family ministry, men's ministry, children's ministry, small groups and various rosters.

Beth worked in the Archives of the Brisbane Anglican Diocese and has volunteered in the Brisbane CMS office for several years.

Two of our daughters have participated in short term overseas missions and presently live and serve the Lord in Brisbane and Toowoomba. *One generation commends your works to another, they tell of your mighty acts. They speak of the glorious splendour of your majesty...* Psalm 145:4, 5 (NIV).

In our fallibility, we have sought to be faithful and obedient to the Lord and leave the outcome to Him. We trust that God has achieved His purposes and that His name has been glorified. *So is my word that goes out from my mouth: it will not return to me empty, but will accomplish what I desire and achieve the purpose for which I sent it.* Isaiah 55:11 NIV.

In reminiscing, it has occurred to us how much God used the All Saints' Youth Club in the lives of other people as well as our own. Tragically, some members of the group appear to have drifted away from the faith but there are others who are cause for great rejoicing. They have God-honouring marriages and their families live for Christ in various parts of Australia. One couple has also been involved in independent ministry in PNG and the Solomon Islands. One of our peers from the later years of youth club has always remained a member of All Saints' and has served in various ways including co-ordinating the local CMS prayer gatherings. Praise the Lord.

May the fig tree blossom and there be fruit on the vine. (with reference to Habakkuk 3:17, 18).

> I am the vine: you are the branches. If you remain in me and I in you, you will bear much fruit; apart from me you can do nothing.
>
> — JOHN 15:5 (NIV)

20

IAN MCGRATH
RECOLLECTIONS OF ALL SAINTS' BOOVAL

| Rev Ian and Glenda McGrath

LOOKING BACK OVER THE YEARS I AM GRATEFUL FOR THE solid foundation that was laid in my life by the saints at All Saints' Booval. Many people there had a positive influence on my life. As a pre-schooler in the early 1960s I attended the kindergarten at All Saints' two or three days each week. Audrey Wallis was the Superintendent and I remember her kindness and love even as a youngster. I remember, as a teenager, Audrey telling me how hard it was for her when her husband died, leaving her with two young children. She shared how God had helped her through the ups and downs of life. God was indeed faithful to her and I know that she was a faithful pray-er for the ministry and people of All Saints' as well as for Glenda and me when we left to go to Sydney.

I came up through the Junior and Senior Sunday Schools and I remember them as fun times, though it may have been trying for the teachers at times. The hall was packed with children every Sunday. The annual Sunday School picnic out at Scott's farm, complete with toffee apples and cream buns, was a great treat. Miss Robey was my teacher for a couple of years and I remember Robyn Mortleman, my teacher in the Senior Sunday School, patiently answering my questions.

When I started high school we used to have a small group, led by Alwyn Rose, that met under our house at Booval Street. Sometimes we would stay in church and Alwyn would chat to us afterwards. The backs of the old pews could be reversed so that we could face each other. One Sunday, Alwyn announced that we were going to learn how to pray aloud. This was a new experience for us all. We started with, "Thank you God for..." and then progressed to longer prayers. I loved the fact that he intentionally taught us how to pray. That is something that I have done with numerous people over the years. Alwyn would often preach in the evening and I loved his passion and enthusiasm for the Lord Jesus.

Every Thursday night, CEBS met. Alwyn Smith, Vince Littleford and Gary Campbell among others, were the leaders. I still have my Page handbook which is all about being a disciple of Jesus along with being a good citizen. To my great surprise I was awarded the Page Cross, the highest award in the Page Degree in 1974, and I was featured in the Queensland Times.

Later I became a leader of the Youth Group. The activity one night was making shaving cream pies. Just before we were about to have some fun trying to plaster the shaving cream pies on someone else's face - who should walk into the carpark but the Rector, Kevin Ellem! The kids looked at me, looked at Kevin, looked back at me and I nodded my head. Quick as a wink Kevin was covered in shaving cream. He took this good-naturedly and joined in the fun.

Growing up in a Christian family was a great blessing. There has never been a day when I have not known that I am safe and secure in Jesus. I learnt this from my parents and from all those who ministered to me in my younger years. My parents also encouraged me to be concerned for Christian missions. My first memory of CMS Summer School was at Port Macquarie. I can remember being in a camp bunk bed and rainwater flowing through underneath the tent and Mum saying to Dad, "Jimmy, we are never going camping again." And we didn't. But we did keep going to Summer School. I'm glad we did because it increased my love for mission. There we heard from serving missionaries and there were always great Bible talks.

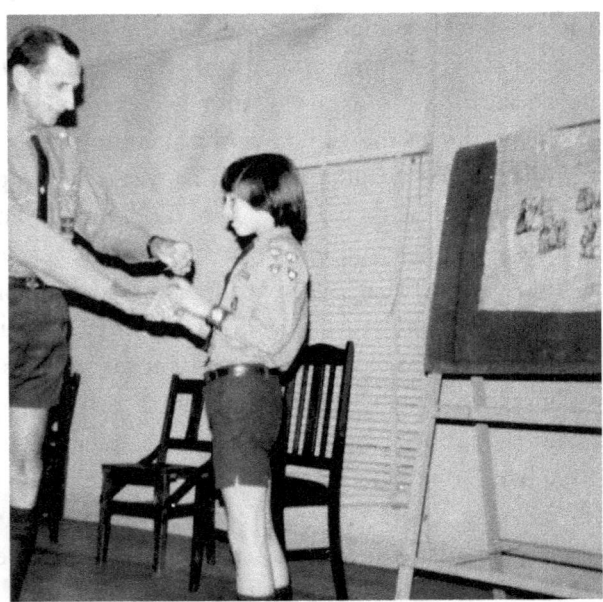

| Ian McGrath receiving the CEBS Page Cross

I remember one Sunday we were having services in the hall because the new All Saints' Church was being built. I was watching Kevin up front on the stage and I was thinking to myself, "I could do that." Then when Rod Irvine was the curate, he said to me one day that I was a leader. That was a pivotal moment for me because I had never thought in those terms before.

I also have fond memories of another curate, Brian Seers. He and I used to play draughts most weekday afternoons and he was often at our place for meals. We had some great conversations about all sorts of things while playing draughts. Looking back, this was a very positive influence in my life.

I'm grateful that Rev Herb Robey and Rev Kevin Ellem both faithfully expounded the Scriptures each Sunday (though it was always a guessing game as to whether the illustration on any Sunday would be about the war or Herb's bike riding - Kevin was far less predictable).

One of the interesting things about All Saints' was that there were always new people coming to the church. I think this was so for several reasons. One was that All Saints' was known as an evangelical Anglican church and so we had people such as John and Annette Nicholls, Peter Friend and Jason Page join us from the RAAF base at Amberley. A second reason was the *Evangelism Explosion (EE)* ministry which my father, Jim McGrath, spearheaded. Many people came to faith through those my dad trained to share the Gospel. Many years later while serving with BCA, it was such a joy to have people come up to me and ask if I was Jim McGrath's son because Jim had witnessed to them and they had become Christians. When I was 17 or 18, I was sitting in our lounge room and Dad was practising his *EE* presentation in the kitchen. As I listened to him, I understood afresh the wonder of the gospel and went on to do the *EE* training myself.

Glenda and I were married in Ipswich in 1983 and soon moved to Sydney where I studied at Moore College. I was the catechist in Cabramatta Parish with Neil and Jane Flower. There were a lot of Vietnamese refugees there and it was the first time that we had worked with people from other cultures. Peter Friend and Jason Page were both at Moore College a year ahead of me. Peter became a chaplain in the RAAF and Jason was ordained in Sydney and later ministered in Canberra.

While at college we reconnected with Don and Margaret Douglass. I could only vaguely remember them from All Saints' since I was very young when they came to Booval. I spent a training week at Ryde Psychiatric Hospital with Don who was Chaplain there. Don had a great love for people and a great love for the Lord. When I saw the way he talked so naturally about Jesus, it seemed to me that Jesus could be sitting in a chair beside him.

In 1986 we moved back to Brisbane and I was a part-time youth minister at Goodna Parish with Frank Savage. Some kids in the youth group were quite a handful. Over 10 years later I received a letter from one of those boys saying that he had become a Christian and thanking us for not giving up on him at the youth group!

At the end of 1987 I was ordained a deacon and we moved to Dalby where Amelia was born. In July 1989 we moved to Bowen where Joel and Isaac were born. I trained a couple of people to do *Evangelism Explosion (EE)*. One night our appointment had been cancelled and I randomly picked someone from the parish roll who lived nearby. I rang and Jane answered and said, "That would be lovely but we are over 80. So don't waste your time, go to someone younger." However, we did visit them and presented the gospel. Dick and Jane with tears in their eyes asked why someone hadn't told them about Jesus when they were younger. The next Sunday and every Sunday thereafter Dick and Jane were faithfully at church growing in the Lord. Another *EE* visit met with rejection by the husband and we weren't able to share the gospel. His wife was a Christian and came to church but he didn't. A couple of months later he received a promotion and they moved to Perth. A year later they were back visiting Bowen and he was at church with his wife. After the service he thanked me for ministering to him because he had since become a Christian. God works in mysterious ways. I think if we sowed more seeds we would see more harvest!

In 1994 we moved with BCA to the parish of the Upper Clarence in Northern NSW. The BCA prayer support was great and made a profound difference. There were 7 centres and Woodenbong was closest to the Queensland border. I called in at the home of a person who had recently moved to town and who was into New Age in a big way. I had an opportunity to share the Gospel with her using *Christianity Explained* and she joined the church there.

In 1996 we moved to Roxby Downs in South Australia again with BCA. It was one of the best places in which we have ever ministered. The Community Church (joint Anglican and Uniting) had people from many different denominations. I used to say to people when they came for the first time, "We have one rule here. We love Jesus and if you don't know Him, then that's a conversation we need to have." We made this the main thing and said to people, "It doesn't matter if you want to dance or wave your hands or cross your arms or sit to sing, as long as you don't expect the other people to do the same as you." Everyone got on wonderfully, no doubt helped by the many people who supported that ministry in prayer.

In 2001 we moved to Moree in north-west New South Wales. It was great to be closer to our family back in Ipswich. In Moree we had lots of baptisms and funerals and these provided points of contact for ministry. Baptism preparation was done in small groups. This helped connect people. I used *Christianity Explained* with them. Then three or four times a year, those people would be invited to do *Christianity Explored* with the Curate while volunteers played with the children and fed them. Through this approach many became Christians and joined the congregation. There always seemed to be plenty of prams at church.

In 2007 we moved to Brisbane to serve with BCA again, this time as Regional Officer for Queensland and Northern New South Wales. As well as speaking in churches and community organisations, I conducted mental health, first aid training and suicide awareness training for parishes and industry across the region. Some community groups were quite explicit that I was not to talk about religion but telling brief stories about the amazing things happening in remote areas through BCA couldn't help but make people think about God.

In 2015 we moved to St Andrew's South Brisbane as the associate priest where ministry is, as always, interesting and fun. Here, as well as throughout my ministry, I acknowledge the influence that growing up in the spiritually dynamic community of All Saints' Booval has had on me. It gave me a good grasp of the Bible and the centrality of the Gospel. It taught me that all kinds of people are welcome at church. It taught me the importance of mission particularly through its support of CMS and BCA.

I thank God for All Saints' Booval.

21

FRANK AND MERLE SAVAGE
JOTTINGS ABOUT ALL SAINTS' BOOVAL

Rev Frank and Mrs Merle Savage

MERLE AND I WERE BORN, SCHOOLED AND MARRIED IN Rockhampton. I had read some of the stories in the Bible but did not know the Gospel. A fellow telephone trainee (a Baptist) told me I was a sinner. I was insulted. Then he gave me a little evangelistic booklet called *The Reason Why*. God used it to convince me that I was indeed a sinner but that God loved me and Jesus died for me. I believed, and gave my life to Jesus. But the Anglican Church in Rockhampton did not provide what I needed to help me grow. Then at age 21, we were transferred to Beaudesert and God sent the Jehovah's Witnesses to me. A few months of weekly studies with them convinced me they were wrong in denying the Trinity, the divine and human person of Jesus, the personality of the Holy Spirit, salvation by faith, life after death and the reality of heaven and hell. But I was still floundering.

Then at age 22 we were transferred to Ipswich. Merle and I, with a new baby, rented a flat near the Ipswich Grammar School. After a few months, I found the Ipswich Christian Bookshop. Miss Jean Foote, the owner, saw that I needed help and strongly suggested that I go to All Saints' Booval. I went. That was an amazing new world to me! People were so enthusiastic about the Gospel! After church, they stood around and talked about Jesus! They met for Bible studies. I thought only JW's did that. In my past church experiences, I had never seen anything like it.

It was as if something came alive in me. It was a new world of Christian experience. But Merle, a nominal Christian, still didn't get it. I began leaving Christian literature from All Saints' around the house. One day she saw a text on the back of a leaflet about John's gospel: *"These things are written, that you may believe that Jesus is the Christ, the Son of God and that believing you may have life in His name."* (John 20:31 NKJV) The Lord opened her heart and mind, and she was converted. Praise God!

Then we bought an old house in Bundamba which suburb was part of All Saints' Booval parish. We became involved in the Sunday School. I began to really learn the Bible better through preparing lessons for the children and reading lots of Christian books. Merle started attending a Bible study run by Jim Stonier in Vince and Elaine Littleford's home. The Littlefords were wonderful friends to us. The study book was *A Summary of Christian Doctrine* by Louis Berkhof - an excellent book to which I still refer! Merle grew rapidly in her faith. We are so grateful for the Christian fellowship and encouragement we received in those days.

At this time the Rev Don Douglass was the minister and Jim Holbeck was away studying at Ridley College. I remember when he came home for holiday once and Don Douglass had him preach to the tiny congregation at Bundamba. That was the first time I think that I met Jim. He preached on 2 Corinthians 3:6: We are not competent in ourselves, but God makes us competent to be ministers because the Spirit's power is in the Gospel of Christ crucified – the new covenant in the Spirit, not the letter - a great truth that I have gradually appreciated more and more over the last fifty years.

Our time at All Saints' was brief, only a couple of years. But it made a life-long impact. I remember Don Douglass stuttering and how he said that he had initially felt that would disqualify him from preaching. But a wise bishop reminded him that God's strength is made perfect in our weakness (2 Corinthians 12:9). I only heard him preach a few times but I was gripped by his fervour and deep faith. The congregation seemed to hang on his every word. I have often used Don Douglass's powerful ministry, despite stuttering, as a sermon illustration over the years. God uses us despite our weaknesses because His power is more clearly seen that way.

Another of his sayings I have never forgotten. The bishop asked him what he would preach in a final sermon before he left a church. He said, "I would preach Christ." The bishop replied, "and Him crucified!" That is pure gold! Don Douglass also said that our preaching has to come out of our devotional life with the Lord. So true!

Riding my pushbike on my way home from work, I sometimes called in on Jim Stonier in his curate's house at the back of the church. He always patiently talked to me and explained more about the Bible to me. I greatly valued Jim's help. Jim's strong emphasis on the power of God's Holy Word, the Bible, has guided me in ministry throughout all the years. God's work is done by God's Word, proclaimed by God's ambassadors and applied to hearts and minds by God's Holy Spirit of Truth.

There was a Spirit of revival at All Saints' Booval. People spontaneously loved Christ, the Bible and each other. My aim in ministry over the years has been to recreate that atmosphere. Only the Spirit of God can do it.

Several men and women were away studying for Christian ministry at that time. I felt called to do the same. Currently, the Rev Herb Robey was the minister. After some uncertainty, we were advised by Rev Jeff Roper to go to Moore College in Sydney. However, there was some further preparation I needed to do. So we went back to Rockhampton for a couple of years for me to complete adult matriculation. There I studied, among other things, Classical Greek and Biblical Hebrew while fellowshipping with some Baptist and Presbyterian friends. Finally I went to Moore College in Sydney. Ultimately, I was ordained in Tasmania and served as Curate at Burnie for a year in 1972. I did further study at Moore before serving as Curate at Maroochydore Anglican parish for a couple of years. We met some wonderful Christian people in all these moves. We needed the grounding in faith that we learnt at Booval from Don Douglass, Jim Stonier, Herb Robey and the congregation.

Then surprise! In 1976 I was appointed as Vicar of Goodna! We were back full circle to an area that had been part of All Saints' Booval Parish. This was a hectic time - 11 years with so much to do - with weekly services at Riverview, Redbank and Goodna. There were many baptisms, weddings, funerals and teaching RE in a number of schools. Contact with old friends at All Saints' was a great support. During this time a major project for us was the sale of the old Redbank Church and the building of the new Collingwood Park Church a few blocks away. Those were years of growth in the congregations with many growing pains for the church and ourselves particularly with 4 children.

In 1987 various circumstances moved us out of the area and out of the Anglican denomination. I was director of Prison Fellowship in Brisbane for a year followed by pastoring a Christian Life Church in Burpengary near Caboolture for 4 years. After postgraduate studies in teaching, we joined the Presbyterian Church and I was called to be minister of Scots Church Clayfield. We were there for about 9 years and again found some fine Christian friends. We have now been serving the Lord Jesus within the Presbyterian denomination for about 30 years - in Queensland, New South Wales, and Victoria. In retirement for the last 11 years the Lord has opened many opportunities for me to continue to preach the unsearchable riches of Christ in various Presbyterian congregations in the south-eastern area of Melbourne. This is a joy to me.

We look back with gratitude to God for the wonderful Christian fellowship and growth we experienced during those few years we spent at All Saints' Booval and especially in the small Bundamba congregation.

May God continue to bless the work at All Saints' for generations to come!

www.ingramcontent.com/pod-product-compliance
Lightning Source LLC
Chambersburg PA
CBHW051403290426
44108CB00015B/2139